When We Gather

A Book of Prayers
for Worship

When We Gather
A Book of Prayers for Worship

Year C

A Collection of Worship Aids
Based on the Lectionary
Prepared for Trial Use
by the North American Committee
on Calendar and Lectionary

James G. Kirk

With art by
Corita Kent

THE GENEVA PRESS
Philadelphia

Book design by Alice Derr

First edition

Published by The Geneva Press®
Philadelphia, Pennsylvania

PRINTED IN THE UNITED STATES OF AMERICA
9 8 7 6 5 4 3 2 1

Library of Congress Cataloging in Publication Data

(Revised for Year C)

Kirk, James G.
  When we gather.

  Includes index.
  Contents: [1] Year A—   —[3] Year C.
  1. Prayers. 2. Liturgies. I. Title.
BV250.K57 1983   264'.051013   83-14221
ISBN 0-664-24505-6 (pbk. : v. 1) (Year A)
ISBN 0-664-24553-6 (pbk. : v. 2) (Year B)
ISBN 0-664-24652-4 (pbk. : v. 3) (Year C)

Contents

Foreword

As contemporary Christians are about the business of being the church, the body of Christ anew in the world, they search for ways to shape and order their lives. One of the ways this ordering of Christian life occurs is through the brilliant work of those responsible for the development of the three-year lectionary cycle. Recognition is given that the Holy Spirit through the Scriptures impresses upon our hearts the love of righteousness. Scripture provides many excellent reasons to bind our hearts to that which is good and of God. Scripture reminds us of God's command to be holy.

> You have seen what I did to the Egyptians, and how I bore you on eagles' wings and brought you to myself. Now therefore, if you will obey my voice and keep my covenant, you shall be my own possession among all peoples; for all the earth is mine, and you shall be to me a kingdom of priests and a holy nation.
> (Exodus 19:4–6)

Scripture further declares that we are reconciled to God in Jesus Christ, who has established for us a pattern of life by which we are to be guided. In Jesus we have a model of openness and humility; he is the faithful and obedient one. Scripture exhorts us to work out our salvation, and to be God's temples surrounded, filled, and flowing with God's love and glory.

The ordered selections of Scripture in Cycle C, accompanied with varied prayers offered here by Dr. James G. Kirk, uniquely help Christians to be about our work of salvation. God's faithfulness to us is evident. All that we need, God has provided. What is our response to be? One way to express our response is in terms of the following seven basic disciplines of discipleship:

To seek God's wisdom which will enable us to be transformed by a renewal of our understanding of God's will.

To seek that which pleases God and exalts God's glory rather than our own.

To deny ourselves presumption, popularity, or pomposity and to seek the things God requires of us.

To seek our neighbors' good as we understand the full implications of the community and fellowship of service.

To seek ways to surrender ourselves and our substance—bane and blessing, pain and pleasure—to God as we bear one another's burdens.

To strengthen our trust in God's love and develop patience and capacity to obey in times of trial and tribulation.

To claim and proclaim the evidence of God's love and light for our lives.

Prayer may be defined as communication with God that clarifies, connects, and compels the human work of God's purpose for our lives. All of the seven disciplines are addressed through Dr. Kirk's relevant prayers: Call to Worship, Prayer of Praise and Adoration, Prayer of Confession, Assurance of Pardon, Prayer of Dedication, Prayer of Supplication, and Prayer of Thanksgiving.

Whether as an individual, a small group, or the corporate body, all who seek to be Jesus' disciples must pray. Any who pray will be inspired and gifted with the expressions written in this volume. After experiencing these prayers, the church will offer gratitude to God for our brother, Dr. James G. Kirk, whose work of Christian love and witness these prayers attest.

THE REV. JOAN SALMONCAMPBELL
Associate Executive
Presbytery of Philadelphia

Preface

The previous two volumes of *When We Gather* have led to invitations to lead workshops on prayer. Inevitably, during these workshops, someone complains that he or she doesn't have time to pray. Either that, or when people have found time, their mind was so cluttered with mundane diversions that they found it difficult to focus on praying.

This resource was born in the struggle to find time for prayer and to learn to focus on one's mind and thought. Like many, I too had little time, and when time was available, random thoughts kept crowding my mind. I was frustrated. I shared my problem with friends. Some suggested retreats, but retreats involve taking more time. Others recommended meditation, but the mind was aware of the many tasks waiting to be done. A discipline was needed, one that each day would focus my thoughts on someone or something other than myself.

When the *Common Lectionary* appeared, I decided to spend time during the week reading the texts suggested for Sunday's worship. On one day I read the psalm. It didn't take long and the psalm itself was a prayer. On the next day I read the Gospel, the next day the Old Testament reading, and the fourth day the Epistle lesson. This pattern continued for a few weeks before I realized what was being done to me.

First, the readings did not leave me throughout the day. Little things would happen to reinforce what had been read earlier. It was as though the moment one dares to open one's self to God's revelation, God enters that life and speaks through the Spirit in practical, daily events.

Second, the need to return daily to the discipline became apparent. When, for whatever reason, I did not read the day's lesson, something was missing throughout the day. There was no sense of having cheated on God. That would bespeak works righteousness, from which Christ frees us. The feeling was more of having cheated myself from the guidance and nurture of God's Spirit. It has been said that the discipline of physical exercise over time becomes addicting. That is to say, if days go by without exercise, the need for it intensifies and must be satisfied. The same might be said of the discipline of reading Scripture. Once begun, it becomes a continuing need.

Third, the time factor took care of itself. I began by taking only the moments necessary to read the text. For a while, that was enough. Soon, without conscious effort on my part, more and more time was spent with the reading. Themes presented themselves. How the texts were linked and why they were chosen for the particular time of the year all became more apparent. The Scriptures suggested decisions that should be made. Where once it was enough to spend four or five minutes reading the text, now thirty or forty minutes passed without notice.

Fourth, the Scriptures themselves offered directions for prayer. The Bible is a rich treasury of metaphor and an essential guide to all the components of prayer: adoration, confession, thanksgiving, and supplication. Since I wanted to learn how to pray, I decided during each four-day cycle of Scripture reading to take notes on suggestions for prayer the texts offered. Then on the fifth day they would be compiled into a prayer for the week. The prayer was repeated on the sixth day, and on the seventh I rested! Within a year the regime was no longer needed, time was not a problem and the mind was focused. The discipline had become an essential part of each day.

The lack of time or the taking of time prevents many people from achieving a disciplined prayer life. It may be due to the fact that time is controllable, a commodity that many North Americans treat like any other commodity. Thus, to approach prayer from the standpoint of how much time it will take or how to fill the time one has taken will prove frustrating. A disciplined prayer life involves allowing God to intrude and transform one's life to God's own glory and praise, regardless of how long it takes.

When We Gather is an example of focusing on the one sufficient revelation of God, Jesus Christ, "the Word of God incarnate, to whom the Holy Spirit bears unique and authoritative witness through the Holy Scriptures, which are received and obeyed as the word of God written." To the extent that the Word of God has been received and obeyed, may God be praised for grace given. The prayers throughout are offered in the firm conviction that Jesus Christ continues to intercede on our behalf when our own words are found to be wanting.

Unless otherwise indicated, Scripture quotations are from the Revised Standard Version. The word "Lord" has been changed to "God," and masculine pronouns for God have been eliminated. In Scripture quoted from the Revised Standard Version, the inclusive word has simply been substituted; in quotations from *The Book of Common Prayer (BCP),* the substituted words are in brackets. In the psalms, the second-person pronouns and their corresponding verb forms have been changed. Material from the Revised Standard Version that has been used in the calls to worship and the litanies has frequently been adapted; for the convenience of the leader of worship, it is not enclosed in quotation marks. In prayers and litanies, Scripture references are given only when the passage cited does not occur in the day's reading.

J.G.K.

Epiphany, 1985

FIRST SUNDAY OF ADVENT

Lectionary Readings for the Day
Ps. 25:1–10; Jer. 33:14–16   *Seasonal Color:*
I Thess. 3:9–13; Luke 21:25–36   *Violet*

A day of great glory is forecast. The people are told to watch for it at all times. Signs will precede its coming, as trees in leaf declare that summer is near. Advent is a time of such expectancy; its sign is a babe full of promise and hope. Therefore, "look up and raise your heads, because your redemption is drawing near."

Call to Worship
LEADER: To you, O God, I lift up my soul. In you I put my trust.
RESPONSE: Make me to know your ways; teach me your paths.
LEADER: Let us worship God.

Prayer of Praise and Adoration
God of redeeming grace, you lead us in paths of righteousness and make your ways known through the birth of a child. We praise your goodness and rely on your wisdom. Accept the sounds of rejoicing we raise to you, and guide our hearing as we seek your instruction. Grant that we may not only worship you joyfully but follow you faithfully all the days of our lives.

Prayer of Confession
UNISON: Great Deliverer, we entrust to you our confession of sin. We are easily discouraged when our good deeds do not make things better. We fear harm to ourselves if we take too firm a stand. Portents of danger arise about us, and we doubt the future you have promised. We close our eyes to the signs and live for the moment. God, in Christ, forgive our cowardice and blindness, for the sake of him who endured the cross for us.

Assurance of Pardon
LEADER: The words of the psalmist remind us that the Sovereign One is upright and good. God instructs sinners in the way of righteousness and leads the humble along paths of steadfast love. So wait upon God all the day long, abide in the covenant, and rely on the truth: God is our salvation and worthy of trust.

Prayer of Dedication

God of promise, you cause the branch of hope to bud and flower; we offer you the fruit of our labor. May what we do bring reassurance to those seeking evidence of your goodness. Use our gifts as signs of what deliverance can mean. We join with the Christ in the struggle for justice; we commit ourselves to the quest for peace.

Prayer of Supplication

Guardian of our lives, it is you who remain faithful when all else falls away. Amid the darkening skies of world events, your vision of righteousness provides a ray of hope. When prophets see empires crumbling, your promise of deliverance sustains us. We trust not in riches, but in your goodness alone to meet our daily needs. You have sheltered your people in the past. We watch for signs of your presence among us still as we endure the trials that continue to confront us.

Grant us a vision of your will to lead us through the unknown morrow. When choices abound, and voices clamor for attention, show us a clear path. We rely on your mercy and would be led by your truth; we yearn to be faithful to the love you have shown.

When we are tempted to waver, help us to step out with confidence. Advent marks a new beginning; we hear anew of the redemption the Messiah brings. Help us embark on faith's journey in spite of risks. When we are alone, comfort us by your Spirit's presence. When we hurt, ease our pain with the healing touch of the great physician. When we are confused because the way is uncertain, speak once more those words of reassurance: "Behold, the days are coming when you shall cause a Branch to spring forth who shall execute justice and righteousness in all the land." For we pray in the name of the one who reveals that righteousness, even Jesus the Christ.

SECOND SUNDAY OF ADVENT

Lectionary Readings for the Day
Ps. 126; Mal. 3:1–4
Phil. 1:3–11; Luke 3:1–6

Seasonal Color:
Violet

The news is out! The messenger is coming! He will bring with him the covenant in which we delight. The valley shall be filled, mountains and hills made low; the crooked shall be made straight, the rough places smooth. Ah, but who can endure the day of his coming? For he will sit in judgment to purify the people until that which they offer is pleasing to God.

Call to Worship
LEADER: Our mouths are filled with laughter; with our tongues we shout for joy.
RESPONSE: You have done great things for us, O God; we come before you with gladness and rejoicing.
LEADER: Let us worship God.

Prayer of Praise and Adoration
You who are a refining fire and a purifying agent, we praise you that in Christ you make us whole again. We gather to hear his coming announced, and anxiously await the dawn of your redeeming grace. Fill our mouths with laughter at the prospect of our liberation, and our tongues with shouts of joy at the news of our redemption. You continue to do great things for us, O God. Therefore we come into your presence with singing.

Prayer of Confession
UNISON: God of abounding grace, have mercy upon us. Our valleys are deep when we are encompassed with care. Our mountains are high when our burdens are heavy. We grope in the maze of our tangled alliances, and reap the pain of bad choices and ignorant gambles. You promised that all flesh shall see your salvation. Show us the straight path and the smooth way that lead to your righteousness, through Jesus Christ, who is the way.

Assurance of Pardon
LEADER: Paul prays that "love may abound more and more, with knowledge and all discernment, so that you may approve what is excellent, and may be pure and blameless for the day of Christ, filled with the fruits of righteousness which come through Jesus

Christ, to the glory and praise of God." Friends, in Christ live in the assurance of righteousness to the glory of God.

Prayer of Dedication

Searcher of hearts, you know our thoughts before they are spoken. You refine our impure acts so they conform to your will. May what we say reflect your purpose for creation, and what we do be consistent with your intent. Shape what we give you to suit your pleasure, and fashion us to fit your design.

Prayer of Thanksgiving and Intercession

O God, you cleanse our tarnished souls and purify our thoughts by the refining fire of judgment; we wait for the day of your messenger's coming, and give thanks for his righteousness by which we are saved from wrath. He walks with us in the valley. He levels the barriers we raise to evade his will. His paths are straight; we need only follow. We can endure the day of his coming, thanks to your mercy; our prayer can be pleasing to you because of his sacrifice for us.

We intercede for those who are despairing. For them the valley seems endless, with no hope of escape. The walls of their own sense of inability close in upon them; they feel alone in their ordeal. Help us to speak the word of comfort and assurance, to offer the embrace of companionship and concern. Together may we smooth the rough places and fill the valleys, so that your will for them may have free course.

We pray on behalf of those encumbered with burdens too heavy to bear. Some of the weight is of their own choosing, some is not. May Christ, who bore our sin upon the cross, ease the burden of all who strain beneath the load. Yoke us with him and with all who are heavy laden, so that together we may complete the task you have assigned to us.

THIRD SUNDAY OF ADVENT

Lectionary Readings for the Day

Isa. 12:2–6; Zeph. 3:14–20

Phil. 4:4–9; Luke 3:7–18

Seasonal Color:
Violet

The prophet proclaims a festival when all God's people will celebrate that God dwells in their midst. It will be a day for rejoicing, for singing songs of salvation, for exclaiming about all the deeds God has done among nations. People in all lands will be united. Peace will be the priority, with judgments erased, enemies cast out, and evil feared no longer, since God will gather all people together.

Call to Worship

LEADER: Behold, God is my strength and my song, and has become my salvation.

RESPONSE: O God, we will give you thanks, call on your name, make known your deeds, and sing your praises.

LEADER: Let us worship God.

Prayer of Praise and Adoration

You put a glad song on our lips, O God of salvation, for in you we can trust and not be afraid. In Christ is announced our source of deliverance; through him the lame walk and the outcast are praised. Soon you will gather your people for a festival of salvation; we assemble now in Christ's name to rejoice and boast of your goodness.

Prayer of Confession

UNISON: Source of salvation, what shall we do? Our lives are unworthy of the goodness you offer. We complain of our condition when our wants go unnoticed. Contentment eludes us, since when we have plenty we still yearn for more. Millions face hunger, while we fret over abundance. Through Christ forgive us, yet grant us no peace until we share our bread with the hungry and our homes with those who lack shelter.

Assurance of Pardon

LEADER: "Rejoice in the Lord always; again I will say, Rejoice. . . . The Lord is at hand. Have no anxiety about anything, but in everything by prayer and supplication with thanksgiving let your requests be made known to God. And the peace of God, which passes all understanding, will keep your hearts and your minds in Christ Jesus." In Christ we are forgiven.

Prayer of Dedication

Gracious God, whatever is true we owe to your mercy. The honorable and just reflect your goodness. When we are pure, it is because you forgive us. Whatever is lovely is a gift of your grace. All of our excellence is due to your kindness. Receive now what we offer as signs of thanksgiving.

Prayer of Thanksgiving and Supplication

Glorious God, we approach you this day with a song in our hearts and praise on our lips. You have chosen to dwell in our midst and bring us salvation. You are the wellspring of all goodness from whom we draw life-giving sustenance. Your glory is manifest throughout creation. We will proclaim to the nations how your name is exalted.

As a warrior in battle, you attack the forces of oppression. Make us as determined to see that justice prevails. Where there is hunger, help us do more than allay it. Give us the insight and conviction to attack its causes. Help us to provide shelter for those who are homeless. Forbid that our warmth should lull us into neglecting their misery. Make us advocates for the voiceless, and a tower of strength for the powerless. Let others see in us a force for justice and peace as we combat whatever keeps your people in chains.

Separate the chaff from the wheat in our lives, and help us to focus on the good we can do and be to your glory. When in response to our baptism we ask, "What shall we do?" make us receptive to the guidance your Spirit provides. The storehouse of our faith is cluttered with well-meaning intentions; many of the past year's resolutions lie forgotten. Remove the gap between our words and our actions as we seek consistency in faith and living. We have offered our prayer; now we commit to you our time and our efforts.

FOURTH SUNDAY OF ADVENT

Lectionary Readings for the Day
Ps. 80:1–7; Micah 5:2–5a
Heb. 10:5–10; Luke 1:39–55

Seasonal Color:
Violet

Two women meet; greetings are exchanged. They are about to be mothers, and have much in common. Elizabeth, full of the Holy Spirit, exclaims that Mary is blessed. Mary, her spirit rejoicing, recites how God has been merciful. Expectation abounds for what is about to occur; those of low degree shall be exalted, and the hungry shall be filled with good things.

Call to Worship
LEADER: Hear, O Shepherd of Israel, . . . stir up your strength and come to help us.

RESPONSE: Restore us, O God of hosts; show the light of your countenance, and we shall be saved.

(BCP)

LEADER: Let us worship God.

Prayer of Praise and Adoration
O Shepherd of Israel, from whom comes forth one who shall feed your flock, we gather as those who dwell in the folds of your embrace and care. Your love envelops us like swaddling cloths wrapped around a babe in a manger. Your countenance shines like a star which led the shepherds one night. We behold your radiance as we enter your sanctuary and praise your name for the Christ who brings us salvation.

Prayer of Confession .
UNISON: Most holy God, in Christ you pour out your mercy to forgive our transgression. Hear us now as we confess our sin. We err in our judgment of what you want from us. We seek to appease you with offerings, earn your favor by doing good deeds, or garner a blessing through making some sacrifice. Forgive us our nature that is prone to buy favor, and in Christ restore us to a right relationship with you.

Assurance of Pardon
LEADER: Micah foresees the Coming One, who shall stand and feed the flock. The people shall dwell secure in the majesty of

God's name. Christ is our peace, and we can dwell secure in the knowledge that through him we are forgiven.

Prayer of Dedication

"Ancient of Days, who sit enthroned in glory, To you all knees are bent, all voices pray." All that we bring you you have bestowed upon us. Whatever good that we do is a sign of your grace. Accept these glad offerings we lay before you as praise for "the goodness that does crown our days."*

Prayer of Thanksgiving and Supplication

Source of salvation, your name is holy. From you comes forth One who shall govern your people. As a shepherd calls the sheep, so will your servant call humanity to come and enter into sanctuary, where they may dwell secure. There they shall be nourished by the word of your covenant, and surrounded with hope that you abide in their midst. Their days shall be spent following the shepherd's command; their nights will pass quickly as they rest secure in your love. We give thanks that we may be numbered among those whom through Christ you have chosen; we seek to be faithful to the call we receive.

We pray for courage to respond to Christ's will in spite of the risk; make us persistent in our ministry as a shepherd in search of lost sheep. Where persons are lost or bewildered, help us to stand as shining rays of hope. To those who wander aimlessly or unsure of themselves, let us bring fresh esteem, clarity of mind, and renewed purpose. To those beguiled by false hopes and vain promises, our prayer is that your Spirit will impart wise counsel and true hope. For those who are pursued and attacked by ruthless forces, we pray for determination and strength to come to their aid.

Make us worthy in all that we do to bear the stamp of your approval and election. Secure in your love, may we be bold in facing the forces of evil. Nourished by your word, may we extend to all Christ's gift of new life. Fill our days with moments that please you, and our nights with the peace of the reconciled.

*The Worshipbook, p. 297.

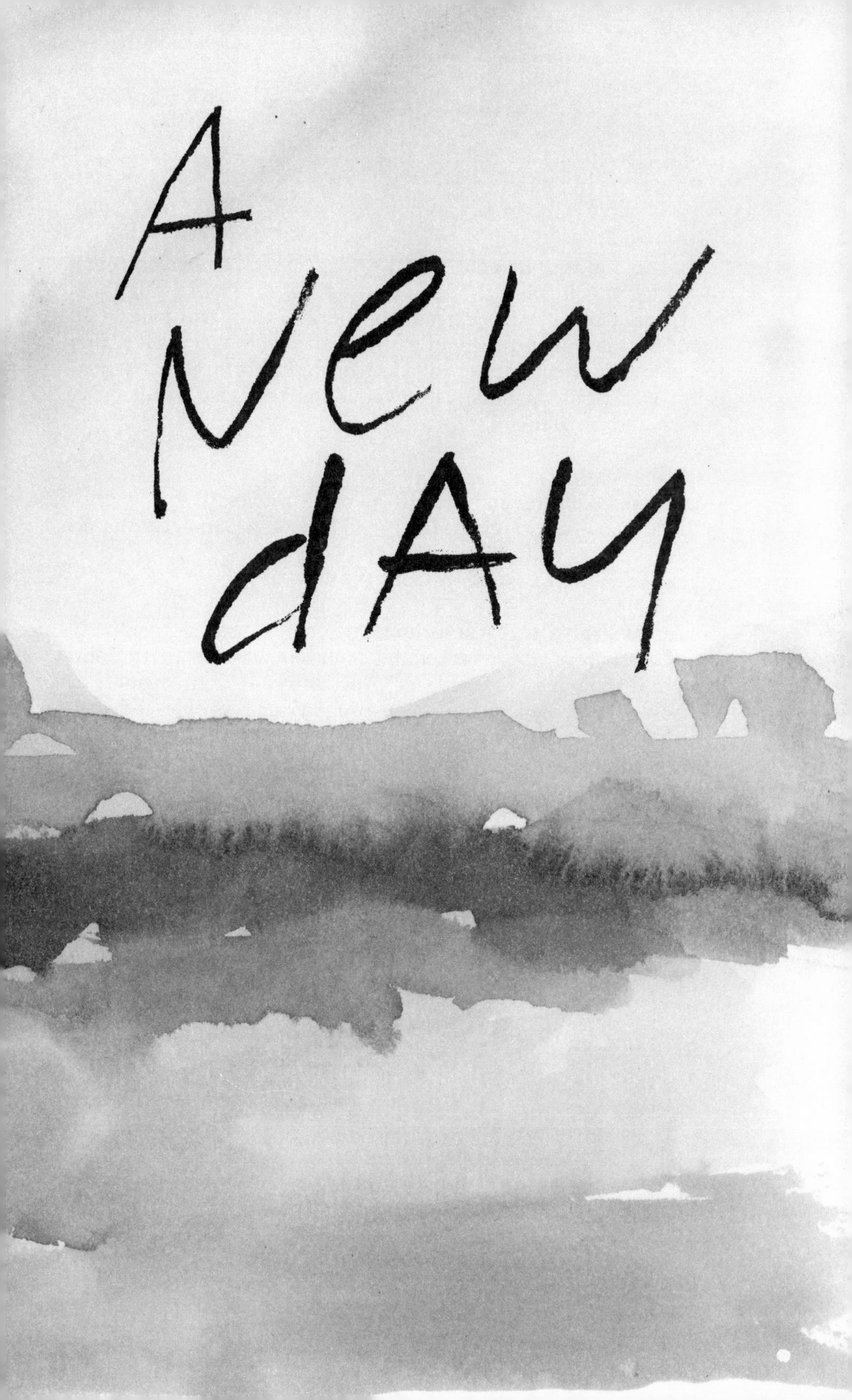
A new day

CHRISTMAS EVE/DAY

Lectionary Readings for the Day
Ps. 97; Isa. 62:6–7, 10–12
Titus 3:4–7; Luke 2:8–20

Seasonal Color:
White

As shepherds watch their flocks, God's glory shines on them; they hear the angel say, "Be not afraid." A star will guide them to where a birth has occurred; full of joy, they will behold an event that promises peace on earth. Today, followers still gather to celebrate what happened: God brought forth Jesus, whose cause was righteousness. The everlasting response has been to rejoice and be glad.

Call to Worship
LEADER: God reigns! Let all the earth rejoice!
RESPONSE: We will rejoice in you, O Holy One, and give thanks to your holy name!
LEADER: Let us worship God.

Prayer of Praise and Adoration
O God, before whom mountains melt like wax, the earth trembles, and idols are humbled, we proclaim your righteousness as we behold your glory. You have sought out a people and proclaimed them holy; you have sent your chosen one, Jesus, to prepare your way. We have passed through the gates of salvation which he opened for us, and now gather to worship you with our praise and thanksgiving.

Litany of Affirmation
LEADER: When the goodness and loving kindness of God our Savior appeared, God saved us.
RESPONSE: So that we might be justified by God's grace and become heirs in hope of eternal life.
LEADER: God saved us, not because of deeds done by us in righteousness, but in virtue of God's own mercy.
RESPONSE: So that we might be justified by God's grace and become heirs in hope of eternal life.
LEADER: God saved us by the washing of regeneration and renewal in the Holy Spirit, which God poured out upon us richly through Jesus Christ our Savior.
RESPONSE: So that we might be justified by God's grace and become heirs in hope of eternal life.

Prayer of Dedication

God of goodness and kindness, whose mercy is from everlasting to everlasting, all that we have are gifts of your grace. As the heavenly host sang of your glory, accept what we bring you as our offerings of praise. With the shepherds we have witnessed the birth of our Savior; our response is in gratitude for the hope of new life we receive in Christ Jesus.

Prayer of Thanksgiving

With "hosannas" we herald the birth of our Savior; we sing of glad tidings, O God our Redeemer. Through a child you have come to bring peace among us; we are reborn with the hope of new life. We hear the angels proclaiming that we need have no fear, for henceforth you shall be with us in Christ, your begotten. We give thanks for your gift of salvation and hope.

We glorify and praise you for making your will known to us. You have opened the gates of heaven to pilgrims such as we. From Jesus we have caught sight of your righteousness and truth; by him we have been taught your commandments and been called to follow in the way of justice and service. You have not forsaken us when we have strayed from his paths of obedience; through him we give thanks for your forbearance and forgiveness.

On this day when all the earth is bathed in the dazzling light of your presence, we give thanks for your Holy Spirit, who continues to guide us. When we are confused, you grant us clarity. In the midst of ambiguity, we can discern the direction you would have us take. When perplexed, you empower us to rise above those forces which would subdue us. Your gifts are immeasurable and will endure when all else fails.

You are the cause of joy which abounds, the source of our righteousness, and the author of hope which dispels shadows of lingering doubt. With the multitude of the heavenly host, we praise you, saying, "Glory to God in the highest, and on earth peace among those with whom you are pleased."

FIRST SUNDAY AFTER CHRISTMAS

Lectionary Readings for the Day

Ps. 111; I Sam. 2:18–20, 26
Col. 3:12–17; Luke 2:41–52

Seasonal Color:
White

Jesus causes his parents some anxious moments. He wasn't where they thought he was, so they search for him. Three days later they find him in the Temple at Jerusalem, amazing those gathered with his understanding and insight. His reason for being there is straightforward and simple: "Did you not know that I must be in my Father's house?" His mother has things to ponder as they go down to Nazareth.

Call to Worship

LEADER: Let the congregation give thanks to God! Praise of God's name endures for ever.

RESPONSE: Great are your works, O God, full of honor and majesty. Your righteousness endures for ever.

LEADER: Let us worship God.

Prayer of Praise and Adoration

We will indeed praise you, O God, and cause your works to be known. Your mercy and grace shall endure forever. As we obey your commandments and abide by your wisdom, we shall proclaim to the nations how you can be trusted. Upheld by the covenant you established, our feet firmly placed on an unshakable foundation, we enter your presence to give you all glory.

Litany of Exhortation

LEADER: Put on then, as God's chosen ones, holy and beloved, compassion, kindness, lowliness, meekness, and patience.

RESPONSE: Above all we will put on love which binds everything together in perfect harmony.

LEADER: Forbear one another and, if one has a complaint against another, forgive each other.

RESPONSE: Above all we will put on love which binds everything together in perfect harmony.

LEADER: Let the word of Christ dwell in you richly; sing psalms and hymns and spiritual songs with thankfulness to God.

Response: Above all we will put on love which binds every-
thing together in perfect harmony.
Leader: And whatever you do, in word or deed, do in
Christ's name, giving thanks to God.
Response: Above all we will put on love which binds every-
thing together in perfect harmony.

Prayer of Dedication

Giver of every good and perfect gift, tribute and glad praises
we bring to you. Let the words of our mouths proclaim the dawn
of redemption Christ inaugurates. Use our talents to spread
abroad the good news of his reconciling love. Accept the gifts we
offer to further his teachings, so that all people may find in him
the abundant life he so richly promised.

Prayer of Thanksgiving and Intercession

Fountainhead of all wisdom, we have come into your courtyard
to sing your praises; within the sanctuary your word is proclaimed. Surrounded by your Spirit, we hear anew the promise
of the covenant, that Christ came to earth so that all could be
saved. We are amazed at how Jesus taught with authority and
marvel at the poignancy and relevance of his words for today.

We pray for teachers who commit their lives to instructing
others how to grow in wisdom, stature, and favor with you and
their neighbors. We remember with gratitude those who have
influenced us in our growing; we give thanks for their patience,
insight, and supportive compassion. They knew how to prod us
when we were lax, support us when we feared to venture forth,
applaud us when the task was completed. Grant those who teach
an insatiable thirst for continuing enlightenment, and the needed
strength to pursue their arduous tasks.

We pray for students who must discipline themselves to the
never-ending quest for truth. Teach them that truth must serve
goodness, and the fear of God is the beginning of wisdom. Give
them a sufficient measure of insight to satisfy their hunger for the
moment, while implanting a craving for further revelation.

Teach us alike to hunger for righteousness and seek to be fed
the bread of life. We give you thanks for Christ's household of
which we are members, for his table around which we gather
with sisters and brothers, and for the sustaining nourishment
which brings us wisdom, growth, and your continued favor.

SECOND SUNDAY AFTER CHRISTMAS

Lectionary Readings for the Day
Ps. 147:12–20; Jer. 31:7–14
Eph. 1:3–6, 15–18; John 1:1–18

Seasonal Color:
White

A new day has dawned brightly, one filled with promise of God's presence on earth. No longer need persons remain estranged from one another. No longer may any claim that God has forsaken them. The nighttimes of existence will henceforth be restful, not fearful; for darkness cannot overcome the light that has come into the world. So, awake, you faithful; prepare to inherit God's reign!

Call to Worship
LEADER: Praise God! For it is good to sing praises to our God; God is gracious, and a song of praise is seemly.
RESPONSE: You send forth your command to the nations, making peace in its borders. Your word runs swiftly; we praise you, O God.
LEADER: Let us worship God.

Prayer of Praise and Adoration
We sing aloud with gladness, O God, raising our voices in praise of your name. You have not withheld your love from us, but sent forth a messiah to deliver us. As Christ came to earth to embody your love, so now we gather as his body to make our joyful response to such wondrous love. Filled with your Spirit, made alive by your presence, we come rejoicing as we greet your new day.

Litany of Affirmation
LEADER: Blessed be the God and Father of our Lord Jesus Christ, who has blessed us in Christ.
RESPONSE: God destined us in love to be God's sons and daughters through Jesus Christ.
LEADER: Because of your faith in Jesus and love toward all saints, I do not cease to give thanks for you.
RESPONSE: God destined us in love to be God's sons and daughters through Jesus Christ.
LEADER: I pray that the God of glory may give you a spirit of wisdom and knowledge.

RESPONSE: God destined us in love to be God's sons and daughters through Jesus Christ.
LEADER: That you may know the immeasurable greatness of God's power working in all who believe in Christ.
RESPONSE: God destined us in love to be God's sons and daughters through Jesus Christ.

Prayer of Dedication

Great Shepherd of the sheep, you feast our soul with abundance and satisfy your people with goodness. We dine on your mercy and are filled by your grace. Having received your gift of Christ our Redeemer, we no longer languish in barrenness but are full of new life. Accept these gifts that we bring you in response to the love you have shown us in Christ.

Prayer of Thanksgiving and Supplication

You who are Alpha and Omega, the beginning and the end, we greet the dawn of redeeming grace with its radiant beams from Christ's holy face. We have passed through the night of doubt and no longer fear that you will forsake us. The One who was with you when you blessed all creation has come as our savior full of your grace and truth. Through him you have assembled those who were scattered, "the blind and the lame, the woman with child and her who is in travail." We gather as those empowered to become your children and give you thanks for this grace upon grace.

There are those for whom each new day is threatening, whose fears block out the vision of your grace. We pray for them: the unemployed and homeless who find no sense of fulfillment. Their days are spent awaiting the call that does not come. Help us to stand with them and be their companions. May their travail be lessened by our support and encouragement. Fill us with resolve to change a society that denies work and the means of life.

Some spend their days in aimless wandering; they can't remember where they have been or where they are going. We pray for those whom society casts aside. Make us impatient ambassadors for your truth and justice, unwilling to tolerate systems that neglect your children.

You are the beginning of goodness and the end of all our striving. In you abides a hope which cannot be denied. You have assembled us as your children; now dismiss us as your agents. You have caused light to shine in our lives; help us to lead others to that light, so that their day may dawn brightly.

they shall be
planted by
of water,
their fruit

like trees
streams
that yield
in season

BAPTISM OF THE LORD

Lectionary Readings for the Day
Ps. 29; Isa. 61:1–4
Acts 8:14–17; Luke 3:15–17, 21–22

Seasonal Color:
White

There are great expectations! One is coming who will baptize with the Holy Spirit and with fire. The threshing floor will be cleared; the chaff will burn with unquenchable fire; good tidings will come to the afflicted. This one will bind up the broken-hearted and set captives free; those who mourn will find comfort. The heavens shall open and all will hear, "Thou art my beloved Son; with thee I am well pleased."

Call to Worship
LEADER: Give glory to God, worship the Mighty One in the splendor of holiness.
RESPONSE: The voice of the Holy One is full of power and majesty. In God's temple we cry, "Glory!"
LEADER: Let us worship God.

Prayer of Praise and Adoration
God of good tidings, you gladden our hearts with your favor. Our ears are attuned to your words of mercy. Wherever we look, we see the signs of your presence: Christ has truly come to set the captives free. Washed clean by your grace and renewed by your Spirit, we put on the mantles of praise and raise our voices in glad adoration: All glory be to you, O God of splendor and majesty, for in Christ we receive the gift of new life.

Prayer of Confession
UNISON: You, who in Christ have assured redemption, hear our confession and forgive our sin. Christ proclaims your goodwill toward all people, yet we pursue vengeance. Those who mourn go uncomforted, as warfare continues in the earth. Captives without number await deliverance while we take freedom for granted. The afflicted await some sign of good news. Amid the ruin of cities and the clamor of protesting voices, we confess our disobedience. Save your people, O God, and cleanse us of our sin, for the sake of your anointed one, Jesus Christ.

Assurance of Pardon

LEADER: Recall John's words, "I baptize you with water; but he who is mightier than I is coming . . . [who] will baptize you with the Holy Spirit and with fire." As we repent our wickedness, Christ, who knows the intents of our hearts, cleanses us of all sin. The threshing floor is stirred and sifted so the wheat can be gathered. May the unquenchable fire of the Spirit purge our beings and prepare us for the reign of God.

Prayer of Dedication

Source of all we have and are, you have sent Christ to save us. We commit our lives to serve him. Your Spirit abides with us as counselor and guide. We offer our actions to be led by her wisdom. The waters of baptism are a sign of your forgiveness. We dedicate our talents as symbols of faithfulness. May what we bring prove worthy of your benevolence to us.

Prayer of Thanksgiving

O God, who spoke as the heavens opened to declare your pleasure in Jesus Christ, we praise you that we are called in his name and find favor in your sight. As your obedient servant, he was baptized by John and received the Holy Spirit. We praise you for our baptism, and that in Christ you seal our adoption as your sons and daughters. We thank you for the Spirit, who abides with us as a legacy of that inheritance, and for mothers and fathers in ages past who were faithful in transmitting your promises to our generation. From them we have received our confessions of faith. With Christ as the cornerstone you form us into a building of God. With Christ as our closest kin, you blend us into one household of faith.

We rejoice in the remembrance of our initiation into that fellowship. You set us apart and named us; the confession of faith was made and we received your divine blessing.

As hands were laid upon us and we joined with sisters and brothers in ministry, so now we commit ourselves again to go into all the world, to proclaim good news and make disciples. Through the grace of our Savior and empowered by your Holy Spirit we will teach them all that you have commanded us—even to the close of the age.

SECOND SUNDAY AFTER EPIPHANY

Lectionary Readings for the Day
Ps. 36:5–10; Isa. 62:1–5
I Cor. 12:1–11; John 2:1–11

Seasonal Color:
Green

A wedding is no time for the wine to give out, but that's what happens. Jesus and his mother are wedding guests, so Mary has a word with her son. As a result, when the steward tastes what he thinks is water from a jar, he finds instead that it is good wine. Usually hosts served the good wine first, and the poor wine last. With Jesus, guests continue to dine on the abundance of God's richest blessings.

Call to Worship
LEADER: Your love, O God, extends to the heavens; your righteousness is like the ever-rolling mountains.
RESPONSE: We shall feast on the abundance of your goodness, O God, and drink our fill of your mercy, O Fountain of life.
LEADER: Let us worship God.

Prayer of Praise and Adoration
Source of delight and rejoicing, you call us to assemble and partake of your banquet. The tables are spread with the abundance of your everlasting grace. Our cups overflow with the drink of new life. With Christ, our host, we join sisters and brothers to sing glad praises for all the wonders you have done.

Prayer of Confession
UNISON: We blend our voices in common confession, O God; you are our hope of salvation. The Apostle teaches that there are varieties of gifts, yet we judge others because they do not fit our mold. There is one Savior, yet we mistrust those who do not believe as we do, and doubt that they are led by the same Spirit. Forgive us for the many ways we sever the parts of Christ's body. Through him reconcile us and pardon our estrangement.

Assurance of Pardon
LEADER: Remember that Christ "is our peace, who has made us both one, and has broken down the dividing wall of hostility." It is Christ who reconciles us "both to God in one body through

the cross."* Through Christ, live in assurance that you are for-given, and be joined together as fellow citizens of God's house-hold.

Prayer of Dedication

God of steadfast love, you give to each a measure of your bounteous mercy; accept what we offer in return as a gift of love from your family here. If it is service, make it pleasing in your sight. If it is wisdom, let it lead others to worship you alone. If it is dollars, multiply their effectiveness. This do, for the sake of Christ, whose gift of himself has made us one.

Prayer of Supplication

God of inspiration and truth, you call us to serve and through your Holy Spirit empower us with varieties of gifts; we praise you for your grace and mercy. Your grace is living water that cleanses us of all impurity; your mercy is fine wine that enlivens our spirits. Renewed by your grace and mercy and made whole by the truth that sets us free, we offer all that we are in obedience to Christ's call.

We give you our knowledge. It was your gift to us in creation, for you implanted within us the taste for inquiry. May what we have learned be used to sustain and ennoble the life of all. Help us to interpret to others the mysteries we have probed. Make our speech intelligible so that others may hear and respond, and help us translate knowledge into action. Endow us with the daring to set challenging goals, and the energy and discipline to attain them.

We give you our ability to heal. May the Spirit of the living Christ continue to infuse us with compassion. May we always be responsive to those in need and sensitive to their unspoken cries for understanding and support. Give hope a name and a face as we move out toward the wounded in our world.

We give you our faith. Through Christ you taught us how to believe. By your Spirit's power we shall never forsake the quest for greater maturity in the Christian life. Make us eager to learn more of what it means to be Christ's faithful disciples. In all things guide us by your Holy Spirit, and make us instruments of your love and truth.

*Eph. 2:14, 16.

THIRD SUNDAY AFTER EPIPHANY

Lectionary Readings for the Day
Ps. 19:7–14; Neh. 8:1–4a, 5–6, 8–10   *Seasonal Color:*
I Cor. 12:12–30; Luke 4:14–21   *Green*

Jesus confesses at Nazareth that God's Spirit is upon him: he has been anointed to preach good news to the poor, release to captives, sight to the blind, and liberty to the oppressed. Isaiah's prophecy is fulfilled in the presence of those who hear him. Be led today by the same Spirit as Christ addresses you, that you may hear afresh the news of liberation.

Call to Worship
    LEADER: Your law is perfect, O God; it revives the soul; your commandment is pure; it enlightens our eyes.
    RESPONSE: Let the words of my mouth and the meditation of my heart be acceptable in thy sight, my rock and my redeemer.
    LEADER: Let us worship God.

Prayer of Praise and Adoration
Your law is perfect, O God, your ways are just. We praise you for Christ, who makes known your word. Gold's value is nothing compared to the salvation you offer; the sweetness of honey is a foretaste of the feast you prepare. Made alive by your mercy and renewed in your Spirit, we come adoring your goodness, O God, our Rock and Redeemer.

Prayer of Confession
UNISON: O God, have mercy upon us, and through Christ forgive our sin. He called the church to be one body with parts to make it function. We sever that one body through suspicion and hostility; we cannot dine around one common table. We divide into separate bodies and pretend to be the church. We take from one another what belongs to us all. By your grace make us one in Christ.

Assurance of Pardon
LEADER: Paul declares that "as the body is one and has many members, and all the members of the body, though many, are one body, so it is with Christ. For by one Spirit we were all baptized into one body . . . and all were made to drink of one Spirit."

Friends, affirm your baptism and be made one in Christ, since in Christ we are forgiven.

Prayer of Dedication

Great God, we lift up our hands to bring offerings to you; we bow our heads in prayer to give you honor; we worship your name with praise and thanksgiving; in Christ you bless us and call us your own. Full of joy in belonging to Christ's holy family, we join with sisters and brothers everywhere in presenting our gifts.

Prayer of Thanksgiving and Supplication

O God of the prophets and the apostles, and of all women and men who speak the truth and do it, we thank you for Jesus, who brought good news to the oppressed and sealed his message with his blood. Now we need no longer mourn, for he is the life. Now we need no longer grope in darkness, for he is the light. Now we need no longer groan in chains, for he is the liberating word.

O God in Christ, you call us to be prophets; give us a clear vision and the courage to make it known. You call us to be apostles; make us eager to be sent, and steady in our mission. You call us to be teachers; give us needed skills of communication. Keep us faithful in the study of your word in Scripture. Make us partners with you in the quest for truth.

You call us to administer the parts of the body; give us the sense of how the whole ought to function. Teach us patience with the weaker members of the body, and above all deliver us from pride of position and arrogance of power. Make us ministers of peace and encouragement, so that the body may remain whole.

We give you thanks for all who help and heal, and perform miracles of ministry. Grant zeal for your church to each of us and love for its unity, so that in your time sisters and brothers everywhere may gather at one table and confess one God of all.

FOURTH SUNDAY AFTER EPIPHANY

Lectionary Readings for the Day
Ps. 71:1–6; Jer. 1:4–10

I Cor. 13:1–13; Luke 4:21–30

Seasonal Color:
Green

It is nice when people speak well of us and marvel at the wisdom we seem to possess. But how quickly initial acceptance turns to suspicion when they hear utterances with which they do not agree. At first, those who heard Jesus thought he was marvelous, but when they understood the implications of his message, they became angry and sought to destroy him. Indeed, "no prophet is acceptable in his own country."

Call to Worship
LEADER: In you, O God, I take refuge; you are my hope and my trust.

RESPONSE: You are my rock and my fortress. I will continually praise you.

LEADER: Let us worship God.

Prayer of Praise and Adoration
Source of all life, you give birth to the nations; we are conceived by your love. You sustain us in the womb of your mercy; we are nourished and grow in the folds of your grace. You have sent Jesus our Savior to deliver us, and have surrounded our days with your Spirit. Through Christ you conceive us as children of the covenant; we gather in his household to give you our praise.

Prayer of Confession
UNISON: If love is patient, why are we irritable? If love is kind, why are we hostile? If love is not jealous or boastful, why do we flaunt our achievements in the presence of others? O God, in Jesus you have shown love which forgives imperfection; only in him can we forsake childish ways. Forgive our lack of love, and have mercy upon us.

Assurance of Pardon
LEADER: Remember that God has done what the law, weakened by the flesh, could not do. God sent Christ in order to fulfill the law. Now we walk according to the Spirit, who bears witness with our spirit that we are God's children. Friends, claim your legacy; we are forgiven.

Prayer of Dedication

O God of faith, we put our trust in you. Source of hope, we are confident you shall never forsake us. Giver of love in ways too countless to be numbered, we return but a portion of what we have received from you. Use our gifts so that others may be assured of new life and enriched by the gift of your Holy Spirit.

Prayer of Thanksgiving and Supplication

Conceiver, Comforter, and Deliverer of all that lives, moves, and has being, we will continually praise you. You conceived a people who call you beloved. You brought them forth from bondage and gave them a name. You comforted them with the seal of your promised covenant; you nurtured them to have hope and to trust in your will. You sent Christ to deliver your people, and by your Spirit gave birth to the body we call the church. We feel the breath of your Spirit upon us and within us, strengthening, encouraging, and impelling to faithfulness. O God, we thank you for our lives, and the inheritance of your love. Lead us to maturity in Christ.

Build our faith, O God, on the rock of Christ's own obedience. We give thanks that he has gone before us to show the way. Save us from hesitation when the path looks forbidding, and from shrinking back when suffering and hardship block our way. Help us to stand firm in the assurance that you will not forsake us. Hope born of faith will sustain us when the journey becomes perilous; though doubt may cause us to stumble, we will not despair. Give us your Spirit of power when our knees are shaking; reassure us by your comforting presence. May the love of Christ we seek to imitate be reflected in our every act. As the imperfect passes away and we draw nigh to your heavenly splendor, let us do so with rejoicing, for in Christ you set us free.

FIFTH SUNDAY AFTER EPIPHANY

Lectionary Readings for the Day
Ps. 138; Isa. 6:1–8 (9–13)
I Cor. 15:1–11; Luke 5:1–11

Seasonal Color:
Green

What does Jesus know about fishing? After all, Peter and his partners toiled all night and caught nothing, and Peter made his living as a fisher. "Let down your nets," Jesus insists, and soon they are breaking with the catch that was taken. The story is told to make a point: henceforth they will follow Jesus, and their catch will be men and women.

Call to Worship
LEADER: I will bow down . . . and praise your Name, [O God], because of your love and faithfulness.
RESPONSE: Though I walk in the midst of trouble, you keep me safe; . . . your . . . hand shall save me.

(BCP)

LEADER: Let us worship God.

Prayer of Praise and Adoration
You are high and lifted up, O God of hosts; the seraphim sing of your glory. Holy, holy, holy, you are the one we adore. The whole earth is full of your splendor; we see all about us signs of your grace. We come into your temple chanting your praises. You are God of steadfast love and faithfulness; hear us as with our hearts we give you thanks.

Litany of Affirmation
LEADER: I delivered to you as of first importance what I also received, Christ died for our sins in accordance with the scriptures.
RESPONSE: By God's grace I am what I am.
LEADER: Christ was buried and on the third day was raised in accordance with the scriptures.
RESPONSE: By God's grace I am what I am.
LEADER: Christ appeared to Cephas, then to the twelve, then to more than five hundred, and to all called as apostles.
RESPONSE: By God's grace I am what I am.

LEADER: God's grace was not in vain; so we preach and so you believe.
RESPONSE: By God's grace I am what I am.

Prayer of Dedication

Holiest of all, you call us to witness your divine splendor; you touch our lips, and with our voices we praise you. You are uplifted, yet you stoop to hear us, cleansing our guilt and forgiving our sin. We are here in response to your calling; we offer our gifts of time, talents, and tithe. Send us forth as your witnesses, so that hosts may know you and give you glory.

Prayer of Thanksgiving and Supplication

You before whose throne the nations shall one day bow in sacred joy, accept the praise we offer now with our whole hearts. You are high and lifted up; we are humbled by your presence. Yet you have crowned us with the jewel of your sovereign love and given Christ to open for us the way into the holiest of all. Your Spirit surrounds us as we wait; our every sense is filled with the wonder of your presence. You are holy and worthy of our praise; accept our sacrifice as in Christ's name we approach your divine majesty.

Let the coal of your sacred word touch our lips and take away our guilt. Loose our tongues to declare your grandeur, and open our mouths to proclaim your goodness to all people. With Isaiah, make us contrite in confessing our unworthiness to speak for you, yet send us forth by your Spirit to bear witness to your judgment and mercy revealed in Jesus Christ.

Make us strong so that we may bear the good news of your love to the ends of the earth. Kindle our zeal with burning brands from the altar of your love; grant that our enthusiasm may ignite the lives of others, so that together we may minister to people whose eyes and ears are yet closed to the word of truth. Through our faithfulness may the coal from the altar touch their lips and make them clean. For the sake of Christ, your faithful one.

SIXTH SUNDAY AFTER EPIPHANY

Lectionary Readings for the Day

Ps. 1; Jer. 17:5–10

I Cor. 15:12–20; Luke 6:17–26

Seasonal Color:
Green

A touch can have healing power; a blessing can work wonders. Jesus used both throughout his ministry. "All the crowd sought to touch him, for power came forth from him and healed them all." When he blessed the poor, they received God's realm; when he blessed the hungry, they were satisfied. So, in Christ's name reach out and touch someone! It may work wonders.

Call to Worship

LEADER: Blessed are those who delight in God's law and meditate on it both day and night.

RESPONSE: They shall be like trees planted by streams of water, that yield their fruit in season. They shall prosper in all they do.

LEADER: Let us worship God.

Prayer of Praise and Adoration

O God, you are like an ever-flowing stream, watering the earth and refreshing creation. We draw from your Holy Spirit life-giving sustenance; we are cleansed of all sin through Christ our Savior. We receive from your word wisdom to guide us; we sing praises to you for your life-giving care.

Prayer of Confession

UNISON: Forgive our vain repetitions, O God of mercy, for our deeds do not match our words of belief. We mouth pious slogans but fail to correct injustice. We claim to be righteous, while practicing bigotry and rejecting others. We glory in your gifts that bring success and comfort, yet we deny neighbors their right to prosper. Help us to confess Christ risen for all people, and forgive our failure to translate faith into action.

Assurance of Pardon

LEADER: Paul writes, "If Christ has not been raised, your faith is futile and you are still in your sins. . . . But in fact Christ has been raised from the dead, . . . so also in Christ shall all be made alive." For I assure you, in Jesus Christ we are forgiven. So live in Christ that all may see your good works and glorify God, who is in heaven.

Prayer of Dedication

God of many deliverances, who in Christ brings soundness of mind, clarity to vision, wholeness of bodies, and wisdom to all we say and do, receive now the fruits of Christ's work in us. May what we give be used to make known Christ's healing presence, so that all may live with assurance of the new life you offer.

Prayer of Praise and Intercession

Merciful Healer, who causes the dawn to break and turns the night into morning, we give you thanks for promised new life. In you is hope which has endured throughout the ages; with you abides the assurance that we are not alone. When perils confront us and cause anxious moments, you ease our unrest with your comforting presence.

There are some for whom daybreak brings foreboding; they are the lonely, the forgotten, the terminally ill. For them the flush of the morning is tinged with the grim reality that confronts them. Help us bring consolation to those known to us, and return to our memory those whom we have forgotten. May we reach out to touch them and remind them we care. When the time comes for some to cross over, may we be their companion until they abide eternally with you.

For others who embark on the day full of promise, we rejoice in their anticipation and give you the glory. Let their laughter be a chorus of alleluias to your mercy, their confidence a tribute to your Spirit within them. May their enthusiasm be contagious, so that we all may become infused with ardor for tasks the day brings. We shall join them and dance through the hours that await us, uplifting others to the new life in Christ.

SEVENTH SUNDAY AFTER EPIPHANY

Lectionary Readings for the Day
Ps. 37:1–11; Gen. 45:3–11, 15
I Cor. 15:35–38, 42–50; Luke 6:27–38

Seasonal Color:
Green

Jesus has a way of expecting the unpredictable. Who would assume we are to love our enemies? To offer the other cheek would just compound the offense. If we gave to all who begged for handouts, would there be anything left to put away for our future? Ah, but Jesus also teaches that God is merciful and will restore abundantly. "For the measure you give will be the measure you get back." Accept the unpredictable, for God can be trusted.

Call to Worship
LEADER: Trust in God, and do good; so you will dwell in the land, and enjoy security.
RESPONSE: We shall be still before God, and wait patiently, refraining from anger and forsaking wrath.
LEADER: Let us worship God.

Prayer of Praise and Adoration
God of Jacob, Leah, and Rachel, you caused a people to journey; they became a great nation. You named your servant Israel, for you would dwell in their midst. You are God Almighty and worthy of worship; we follow our ancestors and assemble to praise you. Be among us to guide us as we honor and adore you, and sanctify our gathering, O God Most High.

Prayer of Confession
UNISON: O God Most High, our bodies are perishable, but you have sent Christ, the promise of our resurrection. Aging limits us, disease burdens us, disabilities undermine our capacity to function. We are frail creatures at best. Yet we glorify these bodies; they are temples we worship. When some threat afflicts them, we are distraught or destroyed. We confess our idolatry. Teach us to number our days to Christ's glory, and forgive our vain worship of ourselves.

Assurance of Pardon
LEADER: Remember that in all things we are more than conquerors because of God's love. "For I am sure that neither death, nor

life, nor angels, nor principalities, nor things present, nor things to come, nor powers, nor height, nor depth, nor anything else in all creation, will be able to separate us from the love of God in Christ Jesus."* In Christ we are forgiven.

Prayer of Dedication

O God, who in Christ taught us how to be faithful, we respond to his instruction, seeking your favor. Be pleased with the offerings we give you; may our actions contribute to the well-being of others. Surprise the offender with our peaceful solutions and startle the beggar by our willing response. For then we shall love neighbors as Christ bade us to do.

Prayer of Thanksgiving and Supplication

Guardian of our lives, you have carried a people in your womb and given birth to a nation. You have fed them and sustained them, watched over their comings and goings, and welcomed them home from their wayward journeys. We thank you that we are heirs of your covenant with that nation and that your beloved Christ has called us to be part of the household of faith.

Take to your bosom those whose journeys are perilous, who venture for a time through uncertain terrain. Embrace them and lead them with your comforting presence; make them aware of your Spirit, who accompanies them in their plight. As they are guided by Christ, who walked the bitter path to Calvary, may their travail give birth to new life, nurtured by hope.

When risk is certain, we pray for those who fear taking steps of faith. Grant them courage to embark on new paths of discipleship, and sufficient training and discipline to follow your will. Place their feet on the firm foundation of your eternal faithfulness, and help them trust your promises.

To those engaged in responding to Christ's sermon, loving enemies and feeding strangers, give support and continuing challenges. Help us to learn from them what bold commitment can mean. As you called Jacob Israel and set apart a people, we join with our ancestors in response to your grace.

*Rom. 8:38–39.

EIGHTH SUNDAY AFTER EPIPHANY

Lectionary Readings for the Day
Ps. 92:1–4, 12–15; Isa. 55:10–13

I Cor. 15:51–58; Luke 6:39–49

Seasonal Color:
Green

A new day was dawning while Jesus walked this earth. Instead of fasting, there was eating and drinking. Indeed, those invited were not usually found on acceptable guest lists. Some folks had questions about what was occurring. How would the new ways blend with the traditional? Would the old be forsaken as the new was embraced? Jesus was splitting the seams of past custom, and change would be the order of the day.

Call to Worship
LEADER: It is good to give thanks to you, O God, to sing praises to you, O Most High.

RESPONSE: I will declare your steadfast love in the morning, and your faithfulness throughout the night.

LEADER: Let us worship God.

Prayer of Praise and Adoration
It is good to give you thanks, O God, and to sing praises to you, O Most High. The dawn is a gift of your abiding mercy; the night passes safely, thanks to your grace. We arise to grant you all glory and honor; we bow down before you and worship your name. We can herald the coming of a new day of faithfulness because of Christ Jesus, in whose name we pray.

Prayer of Confession
UNISON: Let the trumpet sound, O God, and waken us from slumber. The day passes quickly and our time is soon spent. We are caught sleeping when we should be wakeful; there are tasks to be done, fulfilling your will. Forgive our failure to obey your commandments, and our drowsiness when hearing Christ's word.

Assurance of Pardon
LEADER: "Lo! I tell you a mystery. We shall not all sleep, but we shall all be changed, in a moment, in the twinkling of an eye. . . . Thanks be to God, who gives us the victory through our Savior Jesus Christ." Receive the victory over sin that Christ has won, and arise to a newness of life.

Prayer of Dedication

Author of a new day, you have written in our hearts the promise of your unending covenant; we bring now our gifts in response to your word. Translate our faith into acts that please you. Renew our subscription to our baptismal vows. May what we confess lead others to worship you, and our responses accomplish your purpose on earth.

Prayer of Thanksgiving and Supplication

God of all times and places, as rain and snow come down from heaven and water the earth, giving seed to the sower and bread to the eater, so shall your word accomplish its purpose. O Christ, savior of nations and redeemer of peoples, as your word goes forth and returns not empty to you, we give thanks for all who hear your words and do them. O Holy Spirit, giver of life and source of all joy, we break into singing, with mountains and hills, and join with trees in clapping our hands. O blessed Trinity, the cypress shall sprout as a memorial to your mercy and the myrtle shall stand as a sign of your undying love.

As we dine at Christ's table and there receive gifts of bread and wine, we acknowledge your provision for us from day to day, and pray that whatever we have we shall always share.

Your word continues to guide and correct us. We give thanks that we live surrounded by abiding and abundant testimony to your everlasting promise. Keep us from muting your pledge with halfhearted witness or muffling your purpose by disobedient denial.

As your Holy Spirit continues to achieve harmony amid diversity, bring peace and concord to all our acts, that your realm may come, your will be done.

LAST SUNDAY AFTER EPIPHANY
TRANSFIGURATION

Lectionary Readings for the Day

Ps. 99; Ex. 34:29–35   *Seasonal Color:*
II Cor. 3:12 to 4:2; Luke 9:28–36   *White*

As Jesus was praying, he was transfigured. God acted upon him in a way that changed his appearance; a voice spoke from a cloud declaring that Jesus was God's chosen. Prayer did not end when Jesus and the three disciples descended the mountain; its effects would be felt throughout Jesus' ministry. Prayer is an involving process, capable of radically changing our lives.

Call to Worship

LEADER: God reigns; let the peoples tremble! God is en-throned upon the cherubim; let the earth shake!

RESPONSE: We will extol you, O God, and worship at your holy mountain; for you our God are holy!

LEADER: Let us worship God.

Prayer of Praise and Adoration

Great are your works, O Holy One, and greatly to be praised. Not a day passes without our sensing your presence. You appeared in Jesus, removing the veil from your countenance. You spoke through Christ, that we might know your will. Henceforth we shall behold your glory as we are led by your Spirit. Blessed Trinity, we praise your name.

Prayer of Confession

UNISON: Mystery of mysteries, hide not your face from us. Hear our confession and forgive us of sin. We go to the mountains to escape our involvements. We hear your commandments, then hide from their truth. We hide our faces to conceal our identities; Christ unmasks our pretense and strips us of pride. Help us not to be afraid to encounter your presence, and through Christ to stand before you cleansed of our sin.

Assurance of Pardon

LEADER: The truth is this: As the heavens opened, God spoke and proclaimed that Christ was the chosen one; listen to him. Our Savior proclaims that all who truly believe are cleansed of their sin. Friends, believe the good news of the gospel. In Jesus Christ we are forgiven.

Prayer of Dedication

God of Moses and Elijah, of Christ and the disciples, we too could build you booths, but you would not be pleased. We could bring you burnt offerings, but you do not desire them. You ask us to do justice, to love mercy, and to walk humbly with you. We come now before you, placing our lives in your service. Take us, women and men, young and old, to use us as you deem fit.

Prayer of Thanksgiving

God of Moses and Zipporah, Aaron and Miriam, and all who have appeared before you and spoken on your behalf, we give you thanks. Through them you made known the awesome mystery of your transcendent glory. We give thanks for Christ Jesus, who tore in pieces the curtain that separated us from you. In his name we can approach you and call you by name.

We praise you for the hope we can have in Jesus, who walked among earthly folk, transforming all manner of ills into newness of life. When grief besets us we can turn to him to lift our spirits. When burdened with cares, we are assured that Jesus shares the yoke with us. When our own death confronts us we can see on the cross that he too passed victoriously through his time of trial.

We give thanks for the freedom we gain through life in the Spirit. We can arise and shame our captors through our confession of faith; we can lead those who oppress others to change of heart and life. We proclaim aloud the day of liberty for all of your children, with thanksgiving to Christ, who arose victor over all oppressions.

We are transfigured by your mercy and radically changed by your grace. We set our sights now on the ministry that awaits us, whereby the veil of mystery shall be lifted from your face, and all shall know that you are "God with us," at our side always, in Jesus Christ.

you WATER
the earth

and cause
it to BLOOM

FIRST SUNDAY IN LENT

Lectionary Readings for the Day

Ps. 91:9–16; Deut. 26:1–11

Rom. 10:8b–13; Luke 4:1–13

Seasonal Color:
Violet

Jesus was tempted for forty days in the wilderness. It was a test between apparent weakness and presumed power. Satan presumed that Jesus would respond powerfully to what Satan offered, but Satan mistook the meaning of God's power, and of Satan's own power as well. During those forty days, the devil began to comprehend the true power of Jesus' "weakness."

Call to Worship

LEADER: Make God your refuge, the Most High your habitation.

RESPONSE: All who call upon God's name will be saved.

LEADER: Let us worship God.

Prayer of Praise and Adoration

We call upon you, O God; hear our prayer. We raise our voices in glad adoration. You have brought your people out of bondage; you ministered to Jesus when he was tempted by Satan. You know when your people are afflicted, and understand their estrangement when they are alone and dismayed. We pause along our journey of faithfulness to bow down before you and worship your name.

Prayer of Confession

UNISON: O Judge and Redeemer, we come before you, shorn of all pretense and without cause for pride. We care more about bread than our confession of Christ our Savior. We worship many gods and do not serve you alone. We offer bribes to garner your favor; we do not rely on your promised goodwill. Forgive our deceit and grant us forgiveness. Through Christ we repent our sinful ways.

Assurance of Pardon

LEADER: Paul writes that "if you confess with your lips that Jesus is Savior and believe in your heart that God raised him from the dead, you will be saved." John writes that "if we confess our sins, God is faithful and just, and will forgive our sins and cleanse us from all unrighteousness."* Friends, in Jesus Christ we are forgiven.

Prayer of Dedication

Fostered by your tender care and secure in the haven of your redeeming love, we are emboldened to approach you, O God, with our gifts and offerings. May they be used to bring refuge to the aimless, deliverance to the captives, and protection to all who call on your name. For we bring them in Christ's name, our source of salvation.

Prayer of Thanksgiving and Supplication

Great God of the covenant, we bring you our offerings of praise and thanksgiving; your love is a legacy of Christ's death on the cross. You have given us a good land in which to dwell; you surround us with the evidence of your bounteous mercy; our cup overflows with the grace you bestow. You are a God for all seasons; through Christ you have poured out manifold signs of your abiding love.

As Christ was tested by Satan, we too at times face alluring temptation. Help us to recognize the wiles of the devil and withstand the challenge of evil. If bread is the issue, remind us that you provide sufficient for each day. If authority and glory seduce us, help us to recall that the meek shall inherit your promised splendor. If we are led to tempt God by some plunge into a fruitless and perilous venture, restrain us with your outstretched arm.

We confess our abiding faith in Christ Jesus. Help us to enact with our bodies what we proclaim with our lips. Make our hearts receptive to those who seek understanding; with open arms may we embrace the lonely. Make our feet ready to step out on behalf of the lame and the crippled. May what we say and do enable all your people to pursue their pilgrimage of faith with dignity, poise, and conviction. We raise our hands to praise you, O God, as with our voices we herald you Great God of the covenant.

*I John 1:9.

SECOND SUNDAY IN LENT

Lectionary Readings for the Day
Ps. 127; Gen. 15:1–12, 17–18   *Seasonal Color:*
Phil. 3:17 to 4:1; Luke 13:31–35   *Violet*

There is both anger and pathos in Jesus' gospel. Neither is unusual when dealing with matters of faith. Jesus was angry when Herod threatened his mission. He did not want anything to stand in the way of fulfilling God's will. Jesus lamented when his followers and others of faith were persecuted. To believe to the point of conviction was cause for support, nurture, and protection. Jesus sought to provide them all.

Call to Worship
LEADER: If Yahweh does not build the house, in vain the masons toil;
RESPONSE: If Yahweh does not guard the city, in vain the sentries watch.
(JB)
LEADER: But you, O God, in Christ established the church, and in Christ's name we gather.
RESPONSE: And by your Spirit you watch over your people, giving us cause to rejoice.

Prayer of Praise and Adoration
God of the heavenly commonwealth, we praise you for Jesus, who came as your servant; he opened the gates for us to enter your realm. We laud you for the prophets who proclaimed your vision; through them we see clearly what your covenant involves. We give you all honor for what the disciples delivered to us; they taught us to worship you, and to that end we now lift our voices.

Prayer of Confession
UNISON: Beloved God, whose mercy is everlasting and whose grace endures forever, look with favor upon us as we confess our sin. Lift our minds from earthly things to the vision of your heavenly commonwealth. We revel in self-glory; we delight in vain pursuits; we worship the idols of our base desires. Forgive our shortsighted behavior and reconcile us through Jesus to your eternal will.

Assurance of Pardon

LEADER: Sisters and brothers, be assured that our commonwealth is in heaven. From it we await a Savior, who is Christ Jesus, who shall change our bodies into glory, and we shall dwell eternally in God's realm. Trust in Christ, for therein lies our forgiveness.

Prayer of Dedication

Great Shield and Defender, you visited Abram and made him a great nation. You sent to earth Jesus, who called out the church. We join with the hosts who have gone before us, pilgrims on a journey toward your promised land. We pause on the way to give you our offerings, and dedicate ourselves anew to the faithful quest.

Prayer of Thanksgiving and Supplication

O God of Abraham, Hagar, and Sarah, who fashioned a covenant out of promise and hope, we give you thanks that we are numbered among your sons and daughters. Through Christ you have called us and named us; you have made our bodies your temple, and by your Spirit you empower us for ministry.

As you have shown favor to countless before us, make us now fitting citizens of your commonwealth. Discipleship requires discipline; give us determination to set aside time for prayer and study. Amid the pressures of daily life, help us to be quiet so that we can hear you speaking.

Forbid that we should grow complacent about Christ's call to ministry. Shape our endeavors to coincide with your desires, and refine our efforts with the fires of your judgment. When we are lax, invade our consciences, so that we cannot rest until we abide at your side. If we shy away from confronting evil, inspire us to greater efforts to bring you our offerings of justice and peace.

Lead us as you led the Israelites unto the promised land. If you do not build the house, we shall toil in vain; if you do not guard the city, our watch will be worthless. Having called us in Christ, send forth your Spirit to watch over the course of our journey. May what we do be cause for rejoicing, and who we are reflect the radiance and glory of your promise and hope.

THIRD SUNDAY IN LENT

Lectionary Readings for the Day
Ps. 103:1–13; Ex. 3:1–15
I Cor. 10:1–13; Luke 13:1–9

Seasonal Color:
Violet

The themes are repentance and bearing fruit. One leads to the other. To repent is to do an about-face. To bear fruit is to use bestowed gifts for the well-being of others. Both repentance and bearing fruit imply that someone other than we ourselves will influence our behavior. To repent is to obey God. To bear fruit is to serve our neighbor. Therein lies the great commandment.

Call to Worship
LEADER: Bless God, O my soul; and all that is within me, bless God's holy name!
RESPONSE: For as the heavens are high above the earth, so great is God's steadfast love toward those who fear God.
LEADER: Let us worship God.

Prayer of Praise and Adoration
Merciful God, you have set the heavens above us as a sign of your splendor; you water the earth and cause it to bloom. With Christ as the vine and we the branches, our lives can reflect the radiance of your love and glory. Wherever we look we see your benevolence; with the dawn comes new life because of your grace. We gather to worship, praise, and adore you, God of all mercy and joy sublime.

Prayer of Confession
UNISON: O God, our Rock and Redeemer, hear our confession. We worship idols of our own making; when temptation overtakes us we submit to its charm. We find it easier to grumble at hardships than to praise you for mercies we receive day by day. We test you in every way. Yet you promise that you will not test us beyond our endurance. Forgive us when we take advantage of your loving nature, and restore us to communion with you.

Assurance of Pardon
LEADER: Sisters and brothers, remember that "God is faithful, and . . . will not let you be tempted beyond your strength, but with the temptation will also provide the way of escape, that you

may be able to endure it." Christ is the foundation of our salvation; therein lies assurance that we are forgiven of sin.

Prayer of Dedication

Refuge of those who put their trust in you, you seek not vain sacrifice, nor will you hear empty praises. You take delight in contrite hearts that are ready to do your will. Accept our offerings of praise and thanksgiving, mingled with these tangible gifts that we willingly surrender. They are symbols of our response to your call to repentance and our earnest desire to become more faithful stewards.

Prayer of Thanksgiving and Supplication

God of Abraham and Sarah, Isaac and Rebekah, Jacob and Leah and Rachel, Moses and Zipporah, and countless men and women of the promise, you are remembered throughout generations as the God who will be what you will be. We give you thanks that through Christ we can know you. By your Spirit we sense your presence among us, yet we are not consumed. Speak and we shall listen. Send us forth and we shall serve you. Gather us and we shall worship your holy name. All blessing, laud, and honor, great God who was, is, and evermore shall be.

Yet, who are we that you should speak to us? Christ calls us to follow, and we hesitate to do his bidding. Our ears pound with anxieties that afflict us, drowning out the cries of our neighbors. Clear the channels of communication of whatever keeps us from hearing your voice, and make us effective spokespersons of Christ's summons to ministry.

We shall go where you send us and shall strive to do whatever you command. Armed with the mercy that you bestow on us, how can we fail if we but remain faithful? Yet we admit our unworthiness of so great a distinction. Any gifts we have are the result of your grace.

We yearn to please you, O God, as a response to the favor you have shown us. We want our faith to amount to more than casual observance of days and ceremonies. We are sorry for our past which has been less than well-pleasing, and look to a future of absorbing commitment. Through Christ receive us anew as your faithful people.

FOURTH SUNDAY IN LENT

Lectionary Readings for the Day

Ps. 34:1–8; Josh. 5:9–12

II Cor. 5:16–21; Luke 15:1–3, 11–32

Seasonal Color:
Violet

A son takes his share of the inheritance and travels to a far country. There he squanders the wealth until it is depleted. Cast into squalor, he envisions the situation back home; he repents of his wrongdoing and returns to accept his fate. However, instead of rejection he finds a forgiving father who rejoices that his son is alive. The parable describes the ways of God's realm on earth. Whoever is in Christ is indeed a new creation.

Call to Worship

LEADER: O magnify the Sovereign One with me, and let us exalt God's name together!

RESPONSE: I sought the Sovereign One, and God answered me, and delivered me from all my fears.

LEADER: Let us worship God.

Prayer of Praise and Adoration

You are the Sovereign One, O God, and rightly to be blessed. Your name shall ever be upon our lips. You have heard the poor and saved them from trouble. You have enlightened believers; their faces reflect your radiance. Aglow with the splendor of your promised redemption, we rise up to worship you, ruler of nations.

Prayer of Confession

UNISON: We have tasted your goodness, O God, in Christ our Savior. In that name we come asking forgiveness. We confess that we are greedy, while others go hungry. The daily bread you give is not enough; we must indulge our appetites. Our egos need feeding as well; we crave recognition and ignore our neighbors. Show us once more that Christ is our cup and our portion; may we find in him our heart's delight.

Assurance of Pardon

LEADER: Know that whoever is in Christ is a new creation. "The old has passed away, behold, the new has come. All this is from God, who through Christ reconciled us . . . and gave us the ministry of reconciliation." Friends, put on the new being and become ambassadors for Christ, for we are forgiven.

Prayer of Dedication

God of all creation, who caused the manna to rain from heaven, the land to bear fruit, and parched grain to sustain your people, we come bearing gifts in response to your goodness. You are with us in lean times; when the bounty is great we shall not forget you. As in Christ we feed daily on the bread of new life, so through Christ we dedicate ourselves to your abiding covenant.

Prayer of Thanksgiving

Reconciling God, through Christ you have granted your creatures the hope for new life; we praise your name and give you thanks. The old has passed away, behold the new has come. We no longer fear the wilderness, nor aimless wandering, tempted by forces beyond our control. You have sent us a Savior, who has passed through the wastelands, and has borne our sins for us, since we could not escape them ourselves. We herald our adoption as reconciled sons and daughters and approach the dawn of your everlasting covenant with joy in our hearts.

You have opened the doors of your heavenly home and warmly embraced your returning children. Our feet are made light by your Spirit within us; we can run and not grow weary within your gates. We give thanks for your discipline as a wise parent. You have not allowed us to stray too far from your will.

Assured that you await our return from our ventures, we shall be bold while we journey in faith here on earth. We shall strive to be ambassadors of your promised redemption. Armed with the righteousness Christ has won for us, we shall act for justice and reach out in compassion to neighbors. Through Christ hear us as we go forth rejoicing.

FIFTH SUNDAY IN LENT

Lectionary Readings for the Day
Ps. 126; Isa. 43:16–21
Phil. 3:8–14; John 12:1–8

Seasonal Color:
Violet

The house was filled with the fragrance of ointment as Mary wiped Jesus' feet with her hair. Judas objected to this display of affection, since he could have gotten money for the nard she used. He made some objection about how the poor were forsaken, but Jesus quickly saw through his pretense. Legitimate concern for the poor would continue to be a sign of discipleship; the anointing of Jesus was simply the showing of proper respect.

Call to Worship
LEADER: You fill our mouths with laughter, O God; with our tongues we shout for joy.
RESPONSE: You have done great things for us, O God; we come before you with praise on our lips.
LEADER: Let us worship God.

Prayer of Praise and Adoration
Great Guide and Deliverer, you make a way in the wilderness and cause rivers to flow in the desert; we come repeating your name in glad adoration. You have led your people through wastelands where wild beasts and jackals even honor your name. We number ourselves as among those you have chosen. Hear us as in Christ we come before you, declaring you worthy of all worship and praise.

Prayer of Confession
UNISON: God of mercy, hear us as we confess our sin. Power beguiles us and we deem ourselves worthy. Our good works convince us that we can assure our salvation. We heap treasures about us as signs of merit and status, then build elaborate defenses to keep our prizes secure. Forgive the illusion of our own greatness, and in Christ humble us to receive your reward.

Assurance of Pardon
LEADER: Paul reminds us that he counted everything as loss because of the surpassing worth of knowing Christ Jesus his Savior. Through Christ came the righteousness from God based on faith, not personal attainment. From faith came the promise

of resurrection from the dead. Friends, forgetting what lies behind, let us "press on toward the goal for the prize of the upward call of God in Christ Jesus." Therein lies assurance that we are forgiven.

Prayer of Dedication

Giver of every good and perfect gift, if you would be pleased with costly ointments, we would bring them to you. If adornments brought you pleasure, we could make images of you and bedeck them with fine jewelry. But you are not found in images, nor do you wish useless offerings. Accept our gifts of money as tokens of our abiding allegiance and use them in ways that will enhance your dominion; we pray in Christ, the giver of new life.

Prayer of Thanksgiving and Intercession

God of Mary, Martha, and Lazarus, you are full of compassion and abound in mercy. We give you thanks that we dwell in the realm of your grace. You have passed over our sins in sending us Jesus; we have a glimpse of new life through his days here on earth. When he was tempted, you ministered to him. You gave him authority to cast out the demons. When he cried out for guidance you heard him. He placed his life in your hands; he now dwells by your side. We live evermore with assurance that you will never abandon your people; for that comfort we thank you and praise your name.

Hear us as we pray on behalf of those who for some reason cannot trust your benevolence. They struggle in darkness and stumble through life, for they have not accepted the light. Help us to befriend them. Give us the sense to detect what causes their hearts to turn from you, and help us to deal sensitively with the sources of their resistance to your gospel.

We pray on behalf of those whom our culture despises; they must endure hardships that others inflict on them. Through your Spirit give them counsel. Enable us through Christ to bring them comfort. May we like Mary stoop to their need and anoint them with the balm of compassion and care. Empower us with the truth of Christ's resurrection, so that in sharing their sufferings, we may lead them from despair to the hope of new life.

PASSION SUNDAY/PALM SUNDAY

Lectionary Readings for the Day

Ps. 118:19–29; Isa. 50:4–9a
Phil. 2:5–11; Luke 19:28–40

Seasonal Color:
Red

The curtain of the passion play is about to go up. People will cheer and pay Jesus homage, rejoicing and shouting, "Peace in heaven and glory in the highest!" Jesus has been billed as the one who will liberate God's people from oppressive forces. Will he play the role as a warrior, miracle worker, or charismatic leader? No, when the curtain falls, Jesus will have been tried and sentenced.

Call to Worship

LEADER: We give thanks to you, O God, for you are good; your steadfast love endures for ever!

RESPONSE: Open to me the gates of righteousness, that I may enter through them and give God thanks.

LEADER: Let us worship God.

Prayer of Praise and Adoration

We give you thanks, O God, for opening to us the gates of your righteousness. The stone which the builders rejected has become the head of the corner. We dwell as family within Christ's household; because of your grace we have been saved. Morning by morning we shall arise to praise you; day by day we shall be led by your word. Hear our rejoicing and receive our thanksgiving, blessed be Christ our Redeemer!

Prayer of Confession

UNISON: O God of love, who sent Jesus among us, hear our confession and forgive our sin. When we invoke Christ's name for selfish reasons, have mercy upon us. When our faith is convenient and does not lead to commitment, surround us with grace, that we may repent. We are prone to call on you to satisfy our needs; we practice obedience without cost to our comfort. Forgive our leisurely approach to your sacrifice for us as Christ intercedes on our behalf.

Assurance of Pardon

LEADER: Hear Paul's words when he reminds us to "have this mind among yourselves, which is yours in Christ Jesus, who,

... being found in human form ... humbled himself and became obedient unto death, even death on a cross." As we confess Jesus Christ as Savior, God is just and forgives our sin. Therein lies our assurance.

Prayer of Dedication

Glory be to you, O God, for the gift of creation and its bounteous mercies. Praise be to you, O Christ, for redeeming love and the promise of new life. Thanks be to you, O Holy Spirit, for guidance, counsel, and abiding revelation. O blessed Trinity, we honor and worship you in presenting our offerings. Take our lives and let them be consecrated, O God, to thee.

Prayer of Thanksgiving and Supplication

Merciful God, who bestowed on Christ Jesus the name above every name, we bow down before you and give you the glory. Each morning we awaken to the new life you promise; Christ's teachings instruct us throughout the day's course of events. We hear the voice of your Spirit giving counsel and guidance.

Grant us serenity as we pursue routine tasks. Amid the clamor of demands, help us to bow to your desires. We hear the voices of those around us; their opinions affect our judgment about how we should live. When the crowd shouts approval, we are uplifted. When their response is rejection, we feel forsaken and lost. Help us to discern amid the fanfare and fatigue the persistent prodding of your divine will.

When the way is strewn with the garlands of victory, may we give you the praise and thanksgiving due your glorious name. Keep us from hungering for human adulation. Rather, let us seek your favor. You alone enable us to fulfill our ministry. ·

At times, O God, the cross will loom on the horizon. We shall be asked to take on burdens too great to bear. Support us at such times by the strength of your compassion. May the living presence of Christ continue to inspire us as he intercedes for us in spite of our fears. Sustained by the servanthood he assumed on our behalf, we shall face freely and boldly whatever awaits. O God of Easter, glorious is your name in all the earth!

I SAW
And

A NEW HEAVEN
A NEW EARTH

THE RESURRECTION OF THE LORD
EASTER DAY

Lectionary Readings for the Day
Ps. 118:14–24; Isa. 65:17–25

Acts 10:34–43; Luke 24:1–12

Seasonal Color:
White

The time has come for the wolf and the lamb to feed together and the lion to eat straw, like the ox. Former things shall not be remembered, for behold, God has created new heavens and a new earth. In place of weeping shall be rejoicing, and gladness shall reign among God's chosen people. Christ has risen and opened the gates of God's righteousness. Let the people enter and embrace their salvation.

Call to Worship
LEADER: Open to me the gates of righteousness, that I may enter through them and give thanks to God.

RESPONSE: This is the day which God has made; let us rejoice and be glad in it.

LEADER: Christ is risen!

RESPONSE: Christ is risen indeed!

Prayer of Praise and Adoration
God of salvation, you have rolled the stone away and the tomb is empty. Nothing can defeat your love for humankind. The night is passed and with dawn comes new creation; Christ is risen to bring us new life. We herald with gladness your anointing of Jesus and rejoice in your promised redemption from sin. Hear our shouts of glad adoration as we enter the courtyard of your redeeming grace.

Litany of Assurance
LEADER: God anointed Jesus of Nazareth with the Holy Spirit and with power; he went about doing good and healing all that were oppressed.

RESPONSE: Every one who believes in Jesus Christ receives forgiveness of sins through this name.

LEADER: They put Jesus to death by hanging him on a tree; but God raised Jesus on the third day and made him manifest.

RESPONSE: Every one who believes in Jesus Christ receives forgiveness of sins through this name.

LEADER: And Jesus commanded us to preach to the people, and to testify that he is the one ordained by God.
RESPONSE: Every one who believes in Jesus Christ receives forgiveness of sins through this name.

Prayer of Dedication

God of eternal salvation, we come abounding with joy, transformed by your love. Through Christ you have broken the bonds of oppression, removing all barriers to your unending love. You have made us free to give you praise and thanksgiving. You have our undying devotion for the grace we receive. All our lives long we shall call your name blessed and give you the glory for this gift of new life.

Prayer of Thanksgiving

O God, you who lift the veil of darkness, we awaken to the dawn of your glorious splendor. The gates are open and we can enter your dominion; the stone is rolled away and there is life everlasting! Christ is risen and intercedes for us; nothing can separate us from your love.

Trumpets announce your powerful victory; bells ring out announcing your triumph. There is joy in the land, our weeping is ended; the causes of distress have been overcome by your love. "No more shall there be an infant that lives but a few days, or [persons] who do not fill out [their] days," for all shall live as adopted children, inheriting your favor through Christ our Savior.

We bless you for Mary Magdalene, Joanna, and Mary, the mother of James; they were the heralds of good news that first Easter morning. They ministered to Jesus in his time of trial and would not desert him when he was forsaken and lonely. They remind us this day that we should not doubt your benevolence. You will answer before your people call you; while they are yet speaking, you will hear their cries.

Hear our prayers of rejoicing as we enter your realm of redemption. You have fashioned a land flowing with milk and honey, and granted us days in which mercy has no end. Time has been redeemed by your undying presence and all space is sanctified by your inexhaustible grace. We are your Easter people made alive by Christ's rising. Alleluia and hosanna, thanks be unto you!

SECOND SUNDAY OF EASTER

Lectionary Readings for the Day
Ps. 2; Acts 5:27–32
Rev. 1:4–8; John 20:19–31

Seasonal Color:
White

Jesus came bringing peace. He demonstrated peace by the way he lived. He gave peace by the gift of the Holy Spirit. The peace of Christ would dispel all doubt from Thomas. Truly Jesus Christ was God with us! Generations have passed and countless persons have confessed their faith. In Jesus Christ resides the hope that all people may one day dwell together in peace.

Call to Worship
LEADER: Grace to you and peace from the one who is and who was and who is to come, and from Jesus Christ the faithful witness, the first-born of the dead.
RESPONSE: Our God is the Alpha and the Omega, the one who is and who was and who is to come.
LEADER: Let us worship the eternal God.

Prayer of Praise and Adoration
You are the Alpha and the Omega, O God, the beginning and the end of creation. You caused the formless void to burst into splendor, filling space, and revealing your goodness. Your only-begotten, Jesus Christ, came to bring peace and reconcile those who are estranged. We who have been made one gather to praise your goodness, and raise our voices in glad adoration.

Litany of Affirmation
LEADER: We must obey God rather than human authority.
RESPONSE: To God be glory and dominion for ever and ever.
LEADER: The God of our fathers and mothers raised Jesus, who was killed by hanging on a tree.
RESPONSE: To God be glory and dominion for ever and ever.
LEADER: God exalted him at God's right hand as Leader and Savior.
RESPONSE: To God be glory and dominion for ever and ever.
LEADER: Christ brings repentance and forgiveness of sins.
RESPONSE: To God be glory and dominion for ever and ever.
LEADER: And we are witnesses to these things, and so is the Holy Spirit whom God has given to those who obey.
RESPONSE: To God be glory and dominion for ever and ever.

Prayer of Dedication

O God, who sent Jesus, making the nations his heritage, the ends of the earth his possession, all that we have is a gift of your sovereignty. Our wealth is measured by the mercy you have shown us; even life itself is due to your grace. Entrusted by Jesus as stewards of your dominion, we come before you with the fruits of our labor. Accept them as signs of our gratefulness and use them to further your rule over all creation.

Prayer of Thanksgiving and Supplication

Bringer of peace to the nations, we herald the good news: Christ is risen and we are risen with him. We are delivered from thinking of ourselves more highly than we ought, for we were dead in our sins and Christ rescued us. Since Christ broke down walls of hostility which separated us from our brothers and sisters, we are saved to think of others with new appreciation for their gifts and talents. We are saved as part of your eternal plan for all of creation, and united with your people everywhere in one holy communion.

Blend this diverse gathering of believers into one family, who confess one faith and one baptism. Make the peace Christ gave be the sinew that binds us together, the muscle that makes us strong to serve you, the bone that provides the structure for mission in the world. Keep us from petty rivalries, hasty judgments, and all factious elements of life that sap the body's strength.

United in Christ, may we become your agents of reconciliation in the church. Where class and race cause hurtful distinctions, help us to proclaim the rainbow of your covenant promise. Where peoples contend with one another over conflicting ideologies, make us the mediators of their differences. In all that we do, breathe the Holy Spirit upon us, so that we may stand united as sisters and brothers to the glory and praise of your holy name.

THIRD SUNDAY OF EASTER

Lectionary Readings for the Day

Ps. 30:4–12; Acts 9:1–20   *Seasonal Color:*

Rev. 5:11–14; John 21:1–19   *White*

It was a long night for Jesus' followers, a fishing expedition with no fish. At dawn Jesus appeared on the beach, but they didn't know it was he. He showed them where to catch fish and then he cooked some, and took bread and fish and gave it to them —and then they knew. After breakfast Peter received a lesson on obedience: to love Jesus will mean caring for the sheep and tending to their needs. The test of love is faithful service.

Call to Worship

LEADER: Sing praises to God, O you saints, and give thanks to God's holy name.

RESPONSE: God has turned mourning into dancing; we are girded with gladness and will thank God for ever.

LEADER: Let us worship God.

Prayer of Praise and Adoration

Girded with gladness, we come rejoicing. You are God of salvation; we give you praise. When we cried for help you heard us; from out of the pit you rescued us. You have turned our mourning to dancing, loosed our sackcloth and adorned us with favor. We raise our voices in faithful thanksgiving and give glory and honor to your wondrous name.

Litany of Affirmation

LEADER: Worthy is the Lamb who was slain, to receive power and wealth and wisdom.

RESPONSE: To the Lamb be blessing and honor and glory and might for ever and ever!

LEADER: Christ will send you into the city and tell you what you are to do.

RESPONSE: To the Lamb be blessing and honor and glory and might for ever and ever!

LEADER: You are Christ's chosen instrument, called to suffer for the sake of Christ's name.

RESPONSE: To the Lamb be blessing and honor and glory and might for ever and ever!

LEADER: Christ will restore your sight and fill you with the
Holy Spirit.
RESPONSE: To the Lamb be blessing and honor and glory and
might for ever and ever!

Prayer of Dedication

O Lamb of God, who take away the sins of the world, we come
as your chosen instruments, called to serve. By your might we are
empowered to do what you ask of us; with your blessing, we can
rejoice in the gift of new life; to your glory we have been granted
the Spirit's counsel. Receive our gifts of thanksgiving as we give
you all honor and praise forever and ever.

Prayer of Thanksgiving and Supplication

Keeper of the heavenly scroll, who sent forth the Lamb who
shelters us with his presence, we give thanks that through Christ
we may serve you both day and night. It was Christ who was
slain on our behalf, whom you ransomed that we may have life
unbound by the fetters of sin. Through Christ you gathered a
people unto yourself, establishing a household we call the
church. To you who sit upon the throne, and to the Lamb, we give
all blessing and honor and glory and might.

We give thanks for time spent daily in common toil, for work
to be done and the strength to accomplish those tasks set before
us. Transform the common into the holy, and sanctify the scene
of our labors through the presence of your Holy Spirit. May all
that we do serve as a blessing, and the results of our efforts
upbuild your dominion on earth.

As the risen Christ dined at dawn with the disciples, we give
thanks that you grace our tables with your living presence. May
we not take for granted the abundance of food, but use the
strength we gain from adequate nourishment to work on behalf
of the hungry. Let us not rest until there are guarantees that your
children in all nations are sufficiently nurtured. Only then will
the sheep be tended and the Lamb be given blessing and honor
and glory and might.

FOURTH SUNDAY OF EASTER

Lectionary Readings for the Day

Ps. 23; Acts 13:15–16, 26–33   *Seasonal Color:*
Rev. 7:9–17; John 10:22–30   *White*

Jesus speaks of himself as the shepherd. Those who follow him belong to the flock. They hear his voice and obey him. He guides them to pastures where they are nourished; they find protection from whatever could harm them. Nothing can separate those who believe in Jesus from the love of God in whose name he tends the flock of faith.

Call to Worship

LEADER: [God] is my shepherd; I shall not be in want.
RESPONSE: You spread a table before me in the presence of those who trouble me;
LEADER: You have anointed my head with oil, and my cup is running over.
RESPONSE: Surely your goodness and mercy shall follow me all the days of my life,
UNISON: And I will dwell in the house of [God] for ever.
                                                        (BCP)

Prayer of Praise and Adoration

Shepherd God, around whose table we gather, we give you praise. You lead us beside still waters, restoring our souls with your comforting presence. You lead us in paths of righteousness for the sake of Christ Jesus, who died for our salvation. Even though we walk through valleys that threaten us, we fear no evil. We shall dwell in your house all the days of our lives. For that assurance in Christ we give you glory and honor.

Litany of Assurance

LEADER: Brothers and sisters, to us has been sent the message of salvation.
RESPONSE: Salvation belongs to our God who sits upon the throne, and to the Lamb!
LEADER: God raised Jesus from the dead; and for many days Jesus appeared to those who are now witnesses to the resurrection.
RESPONSE: Salvation belongs to our God who sits upon the throne, and to the Lamb!

LEADER: We bring you the good news that what God promised to our fathers and mothers has been fulfilled: Jesus is risen!
RESPONSE: Salvation belongs to our God who sits upon the throne, and to the Lamb!

Prayer of Dedication

God of all nations, tribes, peoples, and tongues, you have redeemed us by the blood of the Lamb; we go into all nations announcing your victory. We confess with our tongues that Christ is risen, pledge our obedience to follow him faithfully, and proclaim your majesty to the ends of the earth. Hear our prayer and accept our commitment, for they are offered in the name of Christ our Savior.

Prayer of Thanksgiving

Shepherd of God, who set the Lamb in our midst to guide us and wipe away every tear from our eyes, we give you thanksgiving, honor, and praise. Our hearts shall not be troubled, for by your rod you guide us; neither shall we be afraid, for with your staff you comfort us. Goodness and mercy shall follow us all the days of our lives, and by your grace we shall dwell in your house forever.

We shall dwell with thanksgiving for Jesus, who keeps us from perishing; he is the door into the fold of your love. When we hunger, he sustains us with the bread of the covenant; he assuages our thirst with the waters of new life. He is the light of the world that chases away darkness. With him we can walk with assurance through the valley of death.

We shall dwell with honor, since you have come to shepherd us; we can no longer stray far from your path. We rest in green pastures and are refreshed by still waters; you set a table before us, reconciling our enemies; you anoint our heads with oil and mark us as your flock.

We shall dwell to praise and worship you faithfully; we shall bow down before you to give you the glory. Led by your Spirit, we shall grow in wisdom and understanding of what it means to be Christ's disciples. We are encouraged by your mercy, enlivened by your grace, and directed by your guiding presence. We are the sheep of your pasture; all honor be to your name.

FIFTH SUNDAY OF EASTER

Lectionary Readings for the Day
Ps. 145:13b–21; Acts 14:8–18

Rev. 21:1–6; John 13:31–35

Seasonal Color:
White

Love is the way to give God glory. Jesus described how that love could occur. Soon Jesus would no longer be with the disciples. His inheritance to them would be the love they received. They were to show that same love to others, thereby continuing to obey Jesus after his departure. The commandment to love one another has been passed down through the ages, setting apart those who follow the Christ. So, love one another and give God glory, even as Jesus first loved you.

Call to Worship
LEADER: God is faithful in words, gracious in deeds, just in all ways, and kind in all that God does.

RESPONSE: My mouth will speak God's praises, and let all flesh bless God's holy name for ever and ever.

LEADER: Let us worship God.

Prayer of Praise and Adoration
O God, you fulfill the desire of all who call upon you; we gather to worship and praise your name. You uphold those who are falling and raise up those who are bowed down. You are faithful in words, gracious in deeds, just in all ways, and kind in all that you do. Your dominion shall endure forever. With our mouths we will give you blessing and honor.

Litany of Affirmation
LEADER: I saw a new heaven and a new earth; for the first heaven and the first earth had passed away, and the sea was no more.

RESPONSE: God is the Alpha and the Omega, the beginning and the end.

LEADER: I saw the new Jerusalem coming down out of heaven from God, prepared as a bride adorned for her husband.

RESPONSE: God is the Alpha and the Omega, the beginning and the end.

LEADER: Behold, God's dwelling is with all people. God will dwell with them, and they shall be God's people.

RESPONSE: God is the Alpha and the Omega, the beginning and
the end.
LEADER: Behold, God makes all things new.
RESPONSE: God is the Alpha and the Omega, the beginning and
the end.

Prayer of Dedication

Living God, who made heaven, earth, and the sea and all that
is in them, we praise you for rains and fruitful seasons. You
satisfy our hearts with food and gladness. Through Christ you
call us to walk in your ways. We offer our gifts as leaven, to
spread the good news of Christ, the bread of life. We renew our
commitment to serve you gladly and to love one another as you
first loved us.

Prayer of Thanksgiving and Intercession

Fountain of life, who alone can satisfy all who thirst after
righteousness, we give you all honor, blessing, and praise.
Through your Holy Spirit you promise new beginnings; former
things pass away as the new day dawns brightly. We shall live
in the light of your trustworthy counsel and be guided by your
wisdom as in truth we call upon your name.

We pray for those who have recently come to the fountain,
confessing Jesus as the source of salvation. Open to them the
vision of your dominion so that they can see clearly how they
ought to respond. Give them clarity of mind as they seek to
choose and decide in ambiguous situations.

We pray for those burdened with sorrow and pain; hear their
cry and hasten to help them. Astonish them with the eternal
presence of Christ their savior who can wipe away tears and
restore wholeness of health. May they find comfort in those of
us who reach out to embrace them. Give them patience to trust
in the promise that you forsake not your own.

We pray for those who seek new beginnings, for whom
Christ's resurrection is assurance that their past is forgiven. Some
thirst after righteousness. Guide them beside living waters, where
they may drink and be refreshed. Others hunger for justice. Lead
them to the table of reconciliation, and nourish them on the bread
of peace. You are the source of all wisdom, compassion, and
reconciliation; through Christ we bless you for hearing our
prayer.

SIXTH SUNDAY OF EASTER

Lectionary Readings for the Day
Ps. 67; Acts 15:1–2, 22–29   *Seasonal Color:*
Rev. 21:10, 22–27; John 14:23–29   *White*

Jesus foretells the coming of the Holy Spirit. The Spirit will teach and cause those who believe to remember what Jesus said. Jesus' promise is joined with the assurance of peace. In the midst of believing, the peace we receive will not be of this world. It will be the counsel of the Holy Spirit, who will make the word of Jesus penetratingly clear.

Call to Worship
LEADER: May God be gracious to us and bless us and make God's face to shine upon us.
RESPONSE: Let the peoples praise thee, O God; let all the peoples praise thee!
LEADER: Let us worship God.

Prayer of Praise and Adoration
All nations on earth shall bless you, O God, for you have redeemed your people and brought them new life. Through Christ you have caused your word to shine on the just and the unjust. By your Spirit your saving power is known by all those who believe. We come confessing that Christ is our savior; we give you all glory for your gift of redeeming grace.

Litany of Assurance
LEADER: In the Spirit I saw the holy city Jerusalem coming down out of heaven from God.
RESPONSE: Let not your hearts be troubled, neither let them be afraid.
LEADER: I saw no temple in the city, for its temple is God the Almighty and the Lamb.
RESPONSE: Let not your hearts be troubled, neither let them be afraid.
LEADER: By its light shall the nations walk; and its gates shall never be shut by day—and there shall be no night there.
RESPONSE: Let not your hearts be troubled, neither let them be afraid.

LEADER: And the rulers of the earth shall bring into it the glory and the honor of the nations.
RESPONSE: Let not your hearts be troubled, neither let them be afraid.

Prayer of Dedication

God of eternity, enthroned in glory, we come before you bringing our gifts. We humbly submit to your sovereign will. You are the source of all righteousness; we offer ourselves as ambassadors for peace. You are the source of justice; we give of our substance to alleviate hunger and want. You are the means by which all the earth shall prosper; we shall go into all nations and bless your name.

Prayer of Thanksgiving and Supplication

Gracious God, who sent Jesus into the world to proclaim peace to the nations and release for the captives, we stand at the portals of your everlasting dominion and behold your glory. We pledge our allegiance to foster your word among peoples on earth.

Led by the Lamb, we carry your lamp into the cities to illumine the dark places. Let the lamp shine on all who struggle in the darkness: the addicted, the homeless, the unemployed, the exploited. Whatever stands in the way of their walking with dignity, help us to remove.

Full of that peace which Jesus gives, we bring the Spirit's counsel to those who are troubled. Open to them the gates of your guidance. We pray for those attacked by real or imagined demons; keep us from compounding their dis-ease with unwarranted judgment, and guide them to discern the cause of their affliction. We pray for those with learning disabilities; surround them by people skilled in stimulating appropriate patterns for growth. We pray for those who are in hospitals and care centers; bless the doctors, nurses, and orderlies who minister to them. We pray for those whom society has forgotten or would rather not remember; burn their plight upon our consciences. Continue to goad us out of complacency through your indwelling Spirit, so that we do not rest until the lost sheep are brought safely into the fold of the Lamb.

SEVENTH SUNDAY OF EASTER

Lectionary Readings for the Day
Ps. 97; Acts 16:16–34
Rev. 22:12–14, 16–17, 20   *Seasonal Color:*
John 17:20–26   *White*

Jesus prays for unity, a unity that portrays God's glory. Such a unity depends upon Christ's indwelling Spirit, which breaks down the barriers that keep people apart. Unity also depends upon faithfully hearing God's word, as believers seek to discern God's will for their lives. Unity expresses itself in loving one's neighbors, reflecting the same concern for others that Christ had for all those in need.

Call to Worship
LEADER: The heavens proclaim your righteousness, O God.
RESPONSE: And all the peoples behold your glory.
LEADER: Rejoice in God, O you righteous!
RESPONSE: And give thanks to God's holy name!

Prayer of Praise and Adoration
Strong Deliverer, righteousness and justice are the foundation of your throne; your lightnings lighten the world, the earth sees them and trembles. Mountains melt like wax before you; Zion hears and is glad because of your judgments. We shall put aside our worship of vain images and cease our boasting of worthless idols. You are God who in Christ came to redeem us; we rejoice and give thanks to your holy name.

Litany of Assurance
LEADER: Christ is the Alpha and the Omega, the first and the last, the beginning and the end.
RESPONSE: The grace of Christ be with all the saints.
LEADER: Blessed are those who wash their robes, that they may have the right to the tree of life and enter the city by the gates.
RESPONSE: The grace of Christ be with all the saints.
LEADER: Jesus is the root and the offspring of David, the bright morning star.
RESPONSE: The grace of Christ be with all the saints.

LEADER: Let whoever hears say, "Come"; let whoever is thirsty come, let whoever desires take the water of life without price.

RESPONSE: The grace of Christ be with all the saints.

LEADER: Jesus testifies to all these things and says, "Surely I am coming soon." Amen. Come, Lord Jesus!

RESPONSE: The grace of Christ be with all the saints.

Prayer of Dedication

O righteous God, we have heard your word, how we ought to obey you; we have confessed our faith in Christ our Savior. Full of your Spirit, we come now bringing our offerings; they symbolize our thanksgiving and reflect our commitment. Accept them and use them to spread the good news of salvation over all the earth.

Prayer of Thanksgiving

Holy God, you have redeemed us by Christ and reconciled us to yourself in him; we are bold to approach you and bless your name. You have not let the follies of humanity hinder your covenant from being enacted; even a cross could not defeat your reconciling purpose. Throughout history you have revealed your gracious benevolence, and led the pilgrims through their perils toward your promised land. Now we stand on the eve of your Holy Spirit's appearance, and the day shall dawn brightly full of counsel and might. So, come, Creator, Spirit, and enliven your children; make known your presence as you hear our prayer.

Washed clean by the blood of the Lamb, we shall don the robes of our baptism and enter the gates of your eternal dominion. We shall walk upright in the truth of your unrelenting assurance that our sins are forgiven. We shall reach the branches of the tree of life and eat of its fruit, no more to die. For in Christ you have banished the flaming sword from Eden; we can claim our inheritance as heirs of your grace.

Jesus, the bright morning star, shall enlighten our pilgrimage. Christ is the key who opens the prison cell and breaks the fetters of suspicion and hate. We shall listen to him and not grow weary in our endeavors; we shall make known your love to the ends of the earth. And may the grace of Christ, which passes all understanding, be with all your saints, even unto the end of the age.

fields murmur

THE DAY OF PENTECOST

Lectionary Readings for the Day

Ps. 104:24–34; Gen. 11:1–9   *Seasonal Color:*

Acts 2:1–21; John 14:8–17, 25–27   *Red*

The nature of God is revealed in the face of Christ. "Whoever has seen me has seen the Father," says Jesus to Philip. To believe in Jesus is to do the works that Jesus does. Whatever the disciples ask in his name will be granted, to give God the glory. The Spirit will guide Jesus' disciples into all truth. A peace that the world cannot give shall be their legacy from the Master.

Call to Worship

LEADER: O God, how manifold are your works! You have made them all in wisdom; the earth is full of your creatures.

RESPONSE: I will sing to God as long as I live; I will sing praise to my God while I have being.

LEADER: Let us worship God.

Prayer of Praise and Adoration

All the earth is full of your glory, O God; the heavens resound in praise of your name. Brooks ramble along the course you designed for them; leaves whisper of your manifold ways; fields murmur as you pass through them; in the skies the thunder sounds its applause. With countless tongues and voices creation welcomes your presence. We join that throng and lift up our chorus, "Praise God, from whom all mercies flow!"

Prayer of Confession

UNISON: God of wisdom and understanding, have mercy upon us as we confess our sin. Your children are scattered; language keeps them apart. Forgive us for the cultural pride that refuses to learn the language of another. Forgive us for the barriers of insensitivity that repel those whom you seek to call through us. By your Spirit's power undo the plight of Babel by the miracle of Pentecost, to the end that all may hear the gospel and praise the risen Christ with one voice.

Assurance of Pardon

LEADER: As God confused the language of all the earth to keep the people from idolatry, so God sent Christ with the universal message of salvation: "Whoever calls on Christ's name shall be saved." Sisters and brothers, trust that name and be assured: in Jesus Christ we are forgiven.

Prayer of Dedication

O God, to you be the glory! We live to praise you; we trust your judgment; in all that we do we seek to obey you. Receive our offerings; they are the gifts of your Spirit. You have wrought the wonders which accompany new life. We shall not shrink from giving you glory, for we are called by Christ to be stewards of what you create.

Prayer of Thanksgiving and Supplication

Living God, with wondrous works and mighty deeds you continue to astound us with your grace and power. Like the rush of a mighty wind you make known your presence, interrupting our complacency, disturbing our lethargy. In hearing the first cry of a newborn, we sense your grace. You dry the tears of those who mourn; you calm the fears of those who face uncertain futures. You amaze us with wonders beyond comprehension; we stand in awe of your majesty and give thanks for your mercy.

Fill us with your Spirit and enlarge our vision. Open our eyes to the future that awaits beyond the scope of our finite perception. Attune our ears to your words of judgment so that we may discern our errors and forsake them. When we pursue courses of action that destroy your creation, correct our mismanagement and harness our greed. When we thoughtlessly make decisions that cause others to suffer, convict us of our cruelty and help us to right the wrongs.

Fill us with Christ and make us more daring. Implant your commandments within us so that we cannot mistake your truth. When we grasp after straws and are tempted to waver, balance our uncertainty with Christ's words of wisdom. When we stumble and fall in our pursuit of justice, strengthen our weak knees and set us on our path again. Alive in your Spirit and armed with your righteousness, we shall run the course you design for us.

TRINITY SUNDAY

Lectionary Readings for the Day
Ps. 8; Prov. 8:22–31

Rom. 5:1–5; John 16:12–15

Seasonal Color:
White

The Holy Spirit's role in the life of the disciples is defined. The Spirit leads believers in the way of God's truth, repeating what the Spirit has heard. The Spirit declares what is to come, guiding believers to behold God's glory and might. The Spirit takes what Jesus proclaimed and translates that message into relevant guidance. Through the Spirit, God's love in Christ is eternally known.

Call to Worship
LEADER: O God, your name is majestic in all the earth; your glory is chanted above the heavens.

RESPONSE: You have crowned your people with glory and honor; we give you all praise in response to your grace.

LEADER: Let us worship God.

Prayer of Praise and Adoration
Creator God, the earth is yours and all who dwell therein; the moon and stars reflect your radiance. You are the potter who fashions works of beauty from the mud, the painter who hangs the rainbow in the sky as the sign of your covenant. We join with those through the ages who have lauded your works of creation and redemption, evermore praising you, and saying, "How majestic is your name in all the earth!"

Prayer of Confession
UNISON: God of justice and love, who take away the sins of the world, have mercy upon us as we confess our sin. We call you God of creation, yet we serve idols of our own making. We confess Christ as our Savior, yet we rely on elaborate security systems for our protection. We claim the indwelling Spirit, yet we abide by our own counsel. Forgive our double-mindedness, and through Christ make us whole.

Assurance of Pardon
LEADER: Through Jesus Christ we have obtained access to the grace in which we stand, and we can rejoice in the hope of sharing the glory of God. "God's love has been poured into our hearts

through the Holy Spirit which has been given to us." Our assurance rests in the triune God, who grants us new life.

Prayer of Dedication

Set apart by your covenant, redeemed through Christ's sacrifice, and renewed by the refreshing winds of your living Spirit, we come bearing our gifts, O merciful God. They are but a portion of earth's treasure you abundantly give us; with them we commit our time and energy to be Christ's faithful servants. Use all that we bring, and all that we are, to bless your holy name.

Prayer of Thanksgiving

Great Designer of the universe, who fashioned creation to give you unending glory, we laud and honor the work of your hands. You gave depth to the waters and set the springs on their course. You shaped the mountains and brought forth the hills. You established the fields and determined the heavens, made firm the skies and fixed the planets in orbit. You commanded the seas to keep their limits and marked the continents where your people would dwell.

We praise you for Christ, your only-begotten, the firstborn of creation to your eternal delight. Christ pioneered salvation through suffering on our behalf; Christ sanctified what you fashioned, purging it with hyssop and making it whiter than snow. Through Christ we can know you and enter the gates of your covenant, hear your word of wisdom and be led by your will.

We thank you for the Holy Spirit, by whom you pour your love into us. Our hearts take delight in your abounding grace. We find hope through the Spirit who grants us endurance, and know that you also suffer when we cry out in pain. Embraced by your compassion, counseled through your judgment, guided by your truth, and mercifully frustrated in our attempts at disobedience, we reaffirm our baptism in the name of the blessed Trinity. Bound by the Spirit as your covenant children, we rejoice in your creation's goodness and graceful redemption.

SECOND SUNDAY AFTER PENTECOST

Lectionary Readings for the Day
Ps. 100; I Kings 8:22–23, 41–43   *Seasonal Color:*
Gal. 1:1–10; Luke 7:1–10   *Green*

The centurion was a person of authority. When he issued commands to those under him, they were obeyed. His authority had its limits, however. He could not heal his slave, and thus he sought Jesus, whose authority was unequaled. "But say the word," said the centurion, "and let my servant be healed." Jesus marveled at the centurion's faith.

Call to Worship
LEADER: Make a joyful noise, all the lands! Serve God with gladness! Come into God's presence with singing!
RESPONSE: We enter your gates with thanksgiving, O God, and your courts with praise! We give you thanks and bless your name!
LEADER: Let us worship God.

Prayer of Praise and Adoration
We lift our voices to bless you, O God; we bow down before you in humble adoration. You are honored among the hosts of heaven; your word spreads throughout the earth. We proclaim you God of all creation who sent Christ to redeem the nations. Filled with your Spirit, we sing in jubilation; we are your people and your love endures.

Prayer of Confession
UNISON: God of all peoples and nations, hear our confession and forgive our sin. We make enemies of strangers when we distrust them. Fear and suspicion keep your people apart. Jesus came to reconcile our differences, yet your people do not dine at one common table. Heal our divisions and overcome our hostility. Unite us in the bond of your encompassing love.

Assurance of Pardon
LEADER: Hear Paul's words when he writes, "Grace to you and peace from God . . . and our Savior Jesus Christ, who delivers us from the present evil age, according to God's will. To God be the glory for ever and ever" in whom abides our assurance of pardon.

Prayer of Dedication

God of gladness, whose steadfast love endures forever and whose faithfulness is to all generations, we are your people and the sheep of your pasture. We rely on you for guidance along faith's journey; you protect us from harm. We shall dwell in the fold of your embracing mercy and give you the honor you are due. Accept our gifts, for all we receive are gifts of your grace.

Prayer of Praise and Supplication

You who keep covenant with all who walk faithfully before you, we give you thanks for Jesus, your Son, in whose name we journey. He came to set the nations aright, and was himself faithful even unto death. He called disciples to follow him. Their pilgrimage is ours today as we take up our crosses. He taught the meaning of sacrifice for others, and yoked us with him in service to you. We carry the name Christian wherever we wander. We give you thanks, O God, for that indelible sign of your unending covenant; we enter your gates with praise and bless your holy name.

Open the doors of your sovereign realm and give us a fresh vision of discipleship's course. Make us eager to embark on whatever path you choose. If the way is strewn with obstacles, level the rough places and keep us from stumbling. If there is more than one road, help us choose aright. When we meet strangers, may we not pass them by, but invite them to accompany us on the trek of faith. Clear the mists ahead so that we can see clearly. May we not abuse the authority that Jesus grants us.

Whatever strengths we have are gifts of your grace. Grant us humility in our relationships with neighbors; help us to see in them a reflection of your unmeasurable goodness. Chasten our judgment of those under us, and quicken our response to those who are above us; make us as willing to give others the same benefit we would expect to receive. You prepare the table before us, O God, and give Christ the place of honor; you invite all of us to partake as faith's reconciling family. To you be the honor and glory forever and ever. Amen.

THIRD SUNDAY AFTER PENTECOST

Lectionary Readings for the Day
Ps. 113; I Kings 17:17–24

Gal. 1:11–24; Luke 7:11–17

Seasonal Color:

Green

A widow's only son had died and the funeral procession was leaving the city of Nain. Jesus saw the procession and had compassion on the widow, touched the bier and told the young man to arise. When the man spoke, the crowd was amazed, glorified God, and declared Jesus a prophet. Compassion, a touch, and newness of life were the trademarks of Jesus' ministry.

Call to Worship
LEADER: You servants of God, praise God's name!

RESPONSE: Blessed be God's name from this time forth and for evermore! From the rising of the sun to its setting, we shall praise God's name!

LEADER: Let us worship God.

Prayer of Praise and Adoration
Who is likened unto you, O God; with whom can you be compared? You are seated on high and look far down upon the heavens and the earth. You raise the poor from the earth, and the needy you lift from the heap of ashes. You visit calamity's child with the gift of new life, promised in Jesus our Christ and Savior. For all the mercy you shower upon us, we give you glory and sing you our praises.

Prayer of Confession
UNISON: Merciful God, forgive us when we discredit the gospel through our actions. When we are frustrated, we blame you for our misfortune. We envy the well-to-do and forget to seek God's realm. Christ taught the meaning of faith, yet we are full of mistrust and are suspicious of your grace. We confess our faith even as we confess our failure. Forgive us our inconsistent behavior, and heal our divided natures.

Assurance of Pardon
LEADER: As Jesus healed the afflicted and restored those who had died, so also through him our sins are forgiven and we are given new life. Awaken to the assurance of your pardon, and arise to the promise of Christ's redeeming grace.

Prayer of Dedication

Like a potter, you fashioned the clay into designs of everlasting beauty. You set the heavens ablaze to your eternal glory. You create the fields and bring forth the harvest; its yield is ours because of your grace. Hear us, O God, as we give you heartfelt praise, and receive our offerings as signs of our love and gratitude.

Prayer of Thanksgiving and Intercession

You who visit the widow in her sorrow and comfort the suffering in their distress, we praise you for your mercy and compassion. Each day brings the knowledge of your reassuring presence; each night your Spirit watches over us. We awake to the dawn of your promised salvation; we rest with the conviction that you will not leave us alone. We are surrounded by manifold signs of your graciousness, for which we praise your name, O God.

Be with all who mourn the passing of loved ones. Help them to find consolation in the outpouring of sympathy on their behalf. Fill the void left by their loss with abiding memories of those who have departed. Assure your servants of Christ's victory over death, that indeed as Jesus rose again, so those who sleep in him will themselves be raised to life eternal.

We pray for those afflicted with illness and pain. Ease their plight through the presence of your Holy Spirit. May they find comfort from arms that embrace them, guidance from hands that reach out to them, kindness in the eyes watching over them, and hope in the actions of all who care for them.

We who enjoy good health and freedom from ills give you the honor and thanks. Our days pass quickly by and we take so much for granted. Teach us to count the hours as a sacred trust from you, and our time on earth as the gift of your benevolence. Make of our bodies vessels for the extension of Christ's healing ministry, and of our souls the receptacles of your divine love.

FOURTH SUNDAY AFTER PENTECOST

Lectionary Readings for the Day

Ps. 42; I Kings 19:1–8

Gal. 2:15–21; Luke 7:36 to 8:3

Seasonal Color:
Green

The woman known as a sinner knew the meaning of forgiveness; Jesus' host, who was a Pharisee, did not. Luke contrasts how both treated Jesus. The woman kissed Jesus' feet and, weeping, anointed them with ointment, while the host did not give Jesus water for his feet, nor greet him with a kiss. She who was forgiven much loved much; he who was forgiven little showed little love. And yet, was not his need for forgiveness as great?

Call to Worship

LEADER: My soul thirsts for God, for the living God. When shall I come and behold the face of God?

RESPONSE: Hope in God; for I shall again praise the one who is my help and my God.

LEADER: Let us worship God.

Prayer of Praise and Adoration

Giver of hope and gladness, who can turn our sorrow into exaltation, we praise you for Jesus, through whom we live anew. Christ quenches our thirst with living water; when we hunger for righteousness, our lives are filled with good things. We abide in the shelter of your love, O God, and raise our voices to worship and adore you.

Litany of Confession and Assurance

LEADER: We know that a man or a woman is not justified by works of the law.

RESPONSE: We have believed in Christ Jesus, in order to be justified by faith in Christ.

LEADER: But if I build up again those things which I tore down, then I prove myself a transgressor.

RESPONSE: We have believed in Christ Jesus, in order to be justified by faith in Christ.

LEADER: I have been crucified with Christ; it is no longer I who live, but Christ who lives in me.

RESPONSE: We have believed in Christ Jesus, in order to be justified by faith in Christ.

LEADER: The life I now live in the flesh I live by faith in the Son of God, who loved me and gave himself for me.
RESPONSE: We have believed in Christ Jesus, in order to be justified by faith in Christ.

Prayer of Dedication

Messenger from on high, we come having heard your word of assurance; you will minister to us during our sojourn of faith. We shall not want, since you continue to watch over us; you will sustain us daily in response to our needs. Accept now our gifts, for they acknowledge your abundance; whatever we offer is due to your grace. Take them and use them to your glory and honor as in Christ's name we pray.

Prayer of Thanksgiving and Supplication

God of the heavenly host, whose ministering angels visit the afflicted, we join the throng who sing your praise. We stand before your judgment seat redeemed through faith in Christ our Savior. We gather as sisters and brothers of your covenant family, called by Christ to obey your will. As we journey in faith, we bear the burdens of our neighbors and so lessen their strain as you have eased ours.

Speak to us as your angel addressed Elijah. When we are afraid, let us know that you are near. There are some who make light of our efforts to be faithful. Help us to hear your guiding words amid the distraction of other voices.

Nourish us for the journey; help us to trust you for all our needs. Feed us with the bread of heaven broken by Jesus; refresh us with the cup of new life. Anoint us with the oil of gladness and make us loving hosts. Show us afresh the joy of forgiveness. Help us to open the doors of your house to passing strangers, that they can enter therein and find rest. Make us unafraid to offer them the water of baptism, whereby they can be cleansed and find life anew.

Through grace you have sought us; in Christ you redeem us. By faith it is no longer we who live, but Christ who lives in us. God of the heavenly host, praise be unto you.

FIFTH SUNDAY AFTER PENTECOST

Lectionary Readings for the Day

Ps. 43; I Kings 19:9–14   *Seasonal Color:*
Gal. 3:23–29; Luke 9:18–24   *Green*

Jesus asked the disciples who they thought he was. Peter answered, "The Christ of God." Immediately thereafter, Jesus outlined the cost of discipleship. Christ would suffer, be rejected, killed, and on the third day be raised. Those who followed him were to deny themselves, take up their own cross daily, and lose their life for Christ's sake. Discipleship today implies the same: self-denial and sacrifice, following Christ's example.

Call to Worship

LEADER: I will go to the altar of God, to God my exceeding joy; and I will praise you with the lyre, O God, my God.

RESPONSE: Hope in God; for I shall again praise God, my help and my God.

LEADER: Let us worship God.

Prayer of Praise and Adoration

O God of light and truth, lead us by your word to your holy hill and to your dwelling. Then we shall come to your altar with exceeding joy and praise you with the lyre, for you are God. The wind cannot contain you, nor the fire consume you; the earthquake fails to encompass your power, for you are God. Speak as you have spoken with your still small voice, and we shall hear and be your people.

Prayer of Confession

UNISON: Infinite Word of truth, breathe upon us the refreshing breath of your Holy Spirit and forgive our transgression. Cleanse our hearts of false doctrine by the winds of righteousness and truth. Purge us by the fires of your eternal judgment and we shall be pure. Shake the foundations of our jealousy and selfishness and cast us anew in the image of Christ Jesus.

Assurance of Pardon

LEADER: Before faith came, we were confined under the law, kept under restraint until faith should be revealed. Now that faith has come, we are no longer under a custodian; for in Christ Jesus we are God's children, through faith. So, inherit the promise of God's pardon through Christ, and live in the assurance that your sins are forgiven.

Prayer of Dedication

Guardian of our destiny, we come in response to Christ's call to discipleship. We offer our sacrifice of praise and thanksgiving with the prayer that you will deem it worthy of your grace. We offer our deeds of goodness; transform them into acts of benevolence befitting your mercy. We offer our treasure; turn it into the means of new life for all.

Prayer of Thanksgiving and Supplication

God of Elijah, Elisha, Miriam, and Naomi, we give thanks that throughout the ages you have revealed your word. You temper us through the fire of your judgment and speak to us in a still small voice. We praise you that you hide not your face from us, and we rejoice in the wisdom of your infinite word.

Startle us with your pervasive Spirit. Disturb our way of living until it accords with your will. Keep us from becoming lulled by the comforts of the consumer society; make us willing to forsake false treasure in order to follow the Christ. When we are tempted to leave the path you choose for us, frustrate our efforts to go our own way.

Continue to guide us through Christ, who calls us. Let the freshness of your wisdom be as poignant as on the day of baptism, when we confessed our faith with ardor and zest. Keep our commitment attuned to the abiding revelation of Christ's teaching, and make us eager to pursue new ventures of ministry.

Continue to comfort us with your embracing tenderness. Surround those who long for your assuring presence. Be with those weakened by disabling diseases, and strengthen those burdened with cares and concerns. We pray for those who through death have lost loved ones. May we communicate to all those near to us your word of compassion which is never far from us.

SIXTH SUNDAY AFTER PENTECOST

Lectionary Readings for the Day
Ps. 44:1–8; I Kings 19:15–21
Gal. 5:1, 13–25; Luke 9:51–62

Seasonal Color:
Green

To follow Jesus implies certain things. It may mean forsaking security in order to go where Jesus calls; decisions may need to be made now rather than after personal affairs are transacted; once you make the choice, there is no looking back. Discipleship means today what it meant when Jesus walked: choose this day whom you will serve.

Call to Worship
LEADER: O God, we have heard with our ears the deeds you perform.
RESPONSE: In God we have boasted continually, and we will give thanks to your name for ever.
LEADER: Let us worship God.

Prayer of Praise and Adoration
We will boast of your presence among us, O God, and magnify your holy name. You still the avenger; you bring low the mighty; you exalt the humble and forget not your own. We are privileged to be numbered among those you have chosen, and through Christ seek to honor you in all that we do. Hear our praises which we raise before you, as in glad adoration our tributes we bring.

Prayer of Confession
UNISON: God of freedom, set at liberty we who are captive, and grant us absolution as we confess our sin. Prisoners by self-interest, we disregard neighbors. We bolster our own egos at others' expense. When slander is rampant, we seldom stop it. When rumors are rife, we seek not the source. Help us to check our destructive ways lest we consume one another, and cause us to use our freedom in more loving ways.

Assurance of Pardon
LEADER: "The fruit of the Spirit is love, joy, peace, patience, kindness, goodness, faithfulness, gentleness, self-control; against such there is no law." We who "belong to Christ Jesus have crucified the flesh with its passions and desires." Therefore, let us

live in love and bear one another's burdens, in the assurance that we are forgiven and made alive in the Spirit.

Prayer of Dedication

O God, you cast your mantle upon us and mark us for ministry in Christ's name; we come before you with our tithes and offerings. We shall put on your cloak of righteousness as a sign to the nations of how you redeem all people; we shall carry the cross of salvation to the far corners of the globe. Accept these gifts as tokens of our commitment, and bless our endeavors as we serve you in Christ's name.

Prayer of Thanksgiving and Supplication

Author and Finisher of our faith, you have set our feet firmly on freedom's foundation; we praise you and give you thanks. Witnesses of old have taught us of the deliverance of God's people from peril. Scripture recounts their covenant promise: You will be our God and we your people. You, O Christ, have sealed a new covenant in your blood and won for us the victory of life everlasting.

Draw us into a right relationship with you and our neighbor. Help us to stand fast by your Spirit and not abuse your trust. Make our inheritance as your sons and daughters a lasting legacy, one that we are eager to pass on to our heirs. Help us by our example to teach them what it means to love you completely and our neighbor as ourselves.

We pray for neighbors both near and far. Give an extraordinary sense of your delivering power to those who live in peril for your sake. Allow them to walk, free from care. Lift from their shoulders the weight of anxiety, and yoke us to them during their time of trial.

There are those for whom freedom is costly: martyrs, prisoners, and the oppressed. Let them not be denied the birthright of your blessing. Give to prisoners the hope that their confinement does not separate them from your mercy. Lift the oppressed and let them glimpse your glory. Set us on the path of freedom's journey and we shall recount what great deeds you have done.

SEVENTH SUNDAY AFTER PENTECOST

Lectionary Readings for the Day
Ps. 5:1–8; I Kings 21:1–3, 17–21   *Seasonal Color:*
Gal. 6:7–18; Luke 10:1–12, 17–20   *Green*

Jesus commissioned those sent out to preach. They were to go in peace and remain only where they were welcome. Their charge was to heal the sick and to proclaim that God's reign was near. Where they were not received, they were not to fret, but shake the dust from their feet and move on. Throughout the ages the task has not changed: Go where Christ sends you and minister to all who are in need.

Call to Worship
LEADER: Give ear to my words, O God; give heed to my groaning. Hearken to the sound of my cry, for to you I pray.

RESPONSE: I enter your house and worship you, O God; lead me in righteousness and make straight your way.

LEADER: Let us worship God.

Prayer of Praise and Adoration
God of the dawn, we arise to the hope of your redeeming grace. God of the dusk, we rest secure in assurance that you neither slumber nor sleep. God of the noonday sun, we dwell in the midst of your unfailing mercy. You are above us, beneath us, and throughout all creation. Through the abundance of your encompassing love we worship and praise your glorious name.

Prayer of Confession
UNISON: You who make all things new, look with mercy as we confess our sin. The seeds of destruction find fertile soil in us; we nurture them to fruition. We pluck the yield and find it delightful; we rejoice in the evil harvest we have sown. Save us from our love of sinning, O God. Teach us to sow to your Holy Spirit, and reap eternal life.

Assurance of Pardon
LEADER: Just as Paul bore on his body the marks of Jesus, so also may we glory in the cross of Christ Jesus. By it the world has been crucified to us and we to the world. So walk by this rule and dwell

in God's mercy, for through the grace of our Savior we are forgiven.

Prayer of Dedication

O God of the heavenly vineyard, in Christ you have sown the seed of our eternal salvation. Through the Holy Spirit you have planted your word of wisdom and might. We are surrounded by countless acts of your graciousness and are empowered in every way by your sustaining love. Receive the fruits of our labors which we lay before you, and bless them to your glory.

Prayer of Thanksgiving and Supplication

Great God of love, in whose name we labor, we give thanks for the harvest of your redeeming grace. You have given us Jesus to guide us in our quest for faithfulness; you have sent your Spirit to enlighten our path. You watch over us as we endeavor to be his disciples, giving us faith, courage, and patience to pursue the course. We confess anew our commitment to obey more completely, trust more fully, honor more faithfully, and praise you more joyously all our days. You are God of our encircling years; we live, thanks to your love.

Bless us, loving God, as we go forth to labor, so that we may proclaim your peace which passes understanding. Amid the strife of nation with nation, help us to be your agents of righteousness, sounding the trumpet of judgment and boldly declaring your sovereignty over all the earth. Amid the turmoil that afflicts our cities, give us courage to confront the causes of hatred and fear, and point to a more excellent way. Within homes torn asunder by suspicion and selfishness, give us skills that can reconcile parents and children, sisters and brothers, and husbands and wives. Wherever we walk, may we plant seeds of your goodness and the vineyards of your unremitting grace.

Garnish our efforts with the flavor of humility which brings you the honor you are due. Keep us from usurping authority in order to build up ourselves, and from pride in self which makes a mockery of your mercy. May we be content that our names are inscribed as servants of your heavenly dominion. Lead us to boast only in your power, to flourish through faithfulness to Christ's high calling, and to triumph in the truth that makes us free.

EIGHTH SUNDAY AFTER PENTECOST

Lectionary Readings for the Day
Ps. 139:1–12; II Kings 2:1, 6–14 *Seasonal Color:*
Col. 1:1–14; Luke 10:25–37 *Green*

A lawyer asked, "What shall I do to inherit eternal life?" He knew what was written but he wanted an example. Jesus replied by telling the story of the good Samaritan. The Samaritan, a foreigner, knew what it meant to show mercy to someone in need; the religious authorities may also have known but did nothing about it. The lawyer learned that quoting the law is not enough; God calls us to acts of mercy.

Call to Worship

LEADER: O God, you have searched me and known me! Such knowledge is too wonderful for me; I cannot attain it.
RESPONSE: Whither shall I go from your Spirit? Or whither shall I flee from your presence?
LEADER: Let us worship God.

Prayer of Praise and Adoration

Most Holy God, you know our every thought and deed; our lives are not hid from you. You dwell in the heights, yet you stoop to hear us; you inhabit the depths, yet you rise to support our efforts to serve you. You encompass the whole of creation, and are yet concerned for our needs. All praise to you, eternal God; we honor and glorify your holy name.

Prayer of Confession

UNISON: God of compassion, we confess before you that we have sinned. We have passed by our neighbors, and ignored opportunities to show them mercy. We have mocked their misery by making excuses to avoid their plight. We who have been taught the law of love practice instead the law of self-interest. Forgive us, we pray, for the sake of Him who came to bind up the wounds of the one by the side of the road.

Assurance of Pardon

LEADER: Hear Paul's words when he writes of God, who has transferred us from the dominion of darkness and to the care of

Christ our Savior. So, walk in Christ's love with assurance of your redemption and forgiveness of sins.

Prayer of Dedication

God of grace and truth, you fill us with the knowledge of your will in all spiritual wisdom and understanding. We seek to lead a life worthy of your calling in Christ. We bring you the fruit, born of your graciousness, with the prayer that it may be fitting of your blessing and glory.

Prayer of Thanksgiving and Supplication

All-knowing God, you discern our thoughts and are acquainted with all our ways; before a word is on our lips, you know it altogether. You lay your hand upon us in the call of Christ our Savior. You fill us with your Holy Spirit, who leads us by your wisdom and counsel. You guide us throughout our journey's length, forgiving our waywardness, equipping us to serve you, and fulfilling our needs. Nothing we can do escapes your eye; there is nowhere we can hide from you. You are within and without, before us and beyond us. O God of our being, we give you praise and thanksgiving.

Hasten the day when our love for you matches your mercy toward us. Enlarge our hearts to the dimensions of your mercy, and help us to return to you a measure of the love you give to us. Purify our souls with your continuing assurance of pardon, and save us from our love of idols and vain display. Strengthen us whereby we may serve you more effectively and glorify your name through obedience to Christ.

Give us the mind of Christ as we look upon our neighbor. Keep us from passing by those whom society overlooks. Plant indelibly on our hearts the plight of the homeless, the forsaken, and the poor. Lend us a portion of your grace as we seek to lift them from despair; cause their fainting spirits to feel the gentle embrace of Jesus our Savior, who came that all may have life and have it abundantly.

NINTH SUNDAY AFTER PENTECOST

Lectionary Readings for the Day

Ps. 139:13–18; II Kings 4:8–17   *Seasonal Color:*

Col. 1:21–29; Luke 10:38–42   *Green*

Martha and Mary were sisters, each of whom had a special gift. Martha was intent on serving Jesus; Mary was content to listen to his teachings. When Martha objected to Mary's seeming disregard of household chores, Jesus gently rebuked her choice of values. At that point in his ministry, Martha's distraction with much serving was not what Jesus needed.

Call to Worship

LEADER: I praise you, O God, for you are fearful and wonderful. Wonderful are your works!

RESPONSE: How precious to me are your thoughts, O God! When I awake, I am still with you.

LEADER: Let us worship God.

Prayer of Praise and Adoration

Great are your works, O God, and greatly to be praised. Before we were born, you knew our inward parts and did knit them together in our mothers' wombs. Our thoughts of you could exceed the sand and they would not suffice to exhaust your wonder. We marvel at the extent of your wisdom and graciousness as we bow down to worship your glorious name.

Prayer of Confession

UNISON: God of hope and glory, through Christ hear our prayer and renew a right spirit within us. Hostility rages and battles continue; warfare is not ended and lives are lost. We yield to suspicion; our envy creates enemies. We confess that Christ came to create a new order, yet we continue complacently to dwell amid strife. O God, have mercy upon us.

Assurance of Pardon

LEADER: Remember that you are chosen by Christ, who reconciles you to God. Christ presents you holy, blameless, and irreproachable before God. Continue in the faith, remain stable and steadfast and do not shift from the hope of the gospel which you heard. For in Christ you are forgiven.

Prayer of Dedication

We lean on the everlasting arms of your mercy, O God, and dwell in the hope of your grace fulfilled. Whatever good that we do we owe to your power within us; the work of our hands is a gift of your love. Nourish our endeavors with your sustaining Spirit and accept our efforts, as in Christ we seek to fulfill your all-encompassing will.

Prayer of Thanksgiving and Supplication

Giver of life, who conceived creation's dawning and implanted the seeds of your eternal dominion, wonderful are your works and greatly to be praised. You are compassionate and lovingly embrace your creatures. You conceived their well-being and bore the Christ for them. You labored with their sinfulness and sent forth the Spirit. You did not forsake them when death's darkness enshrouded the earth. We live today, thanks to your love.

Hope of the world, we rely on your mercy. Continue to grant us hospice where we can live secure from harm. Help us to find in Christ the anchor of our faith, the haven of calm waters amid unsettling times. Root us and ground us in his teachings, so that when the winds blow, we remain steadfast; when stormy seas threaten, we do not desert you; when we are tossed to and fro, we may remain upright in the conviction that Christ died to free us from ultimate destruction.

Custodian of the future, we depend on your grace. Blend our thoughts with your thoughts. Leaven this lump of creation we call our existence, so that our days on earth reflect your splendor. Renew us with your Holy Spirit and align all that we do with your will for us. When we are depressed, be with us to uplift us; when we stray from your desire, frustrate our errant behavior; when our feet are light, dance with us; when we shout with joy, hear our praise. You have formed our days before we knew they existed. How precious to us are your thoughts, O God. How vast is the sum of them.

TENTH SUNDAY AFTER PENTECOST

Lectionary Readings for the Day

Ps. 21:1–7; II Kings 5:1–15ab

Col. 2:6–15; Luke 11:1–13

Seasonal Color:
Green

Jesus taught his disciples how to pray. First, hallow God's name and let God reign. Thereafter, pray daily for what you need to sustain you and seek forgiveness for the wrongs you have done. Keep away from temptations, since they lead to disobedience. Remember, above all, that God is faithful; God sends the Holy Spirit to fulfill every need.

Call to Worship

LEADER: Whoever asks God for life, God gives it. God bestows splendor and majesty upon all who call on God's name.

RESPONSE: Yea, God makes humanity blessed for ever; we are made glad with the joy of God's presence.

LEADER: Let us worship God.

Prayer of Praise and Adoration

You make us glad with the joy of your presence, O God, and fill our days with your steadfast love. Day by day you meet us with goodly blessings; night after night your steadfast love upholds us. Your glory is great; your help is unfailing. We bow before your splendor and majesty, and praise your name.

Litany of Assurance

LEADER: In Christ the whole fulness of deity dwells bodily, and you have come to fulness of life in Christ.

RESPONSE: As therefore you received Christ Jesus, abound in thanksgiving.

LEADER: You were buried with Christ in baptism and were raised with Christ through faith in the working of God.

RESPONSE: As therefore you received Christ Jesus, abound in thanksgiving.

LEADER: You, who were dead in trespasses, God made alive together with Christ, having forgiven us all our trespasses.

RESPONSE: As therefore you received Christ Jesus, abound in thanksgiving.

LEADER: God disarmed the principalities and powers and made a public example of them, triumphing over them in Christ.

RESPONSE: As therefore you received Christ Jesus, abound in thanksgiving.

Prayer of Dedication

Abounding in hope, we come before you, O God; you are deliverance and life divine. You build a storehouse of goodly blessings and set us within it to sample your love. Whatever our needs, you meet them completely; you surround us with your compassion and care. Receive the offerings that we lay before you. We dedicate all our possessions to your continuing glory.

Prayer of Praise and Supplication

Giver of countless blessings, your reign is divine. Your dominion exceeds the widest expanse of the oceans; your love extends beyond the heavens. Hallowed be your name unto the eternal ages, for you have decreed that you alone are God. Hasten the day when all people shall know you, and let us be agents in proclaiming your will. Make of us stewards who tend your creation; help us teach others how to live at peace with the earth.

Give to us daily what we need to sustain us. Save us from greed and wanton desire. Deliver us from love of goods, the material things we tend to venerate and adore. Help us to be satisfied with the fortunes you heap on us, the grace, mercy, and peace only you can bestow.

We sin in spite of Christ's atoning sacrifice. Bathe us with assurance of Christ's redeeming love. When we judge others unfit for forgiveness, make us mindful of our own need for pardon. Give us a reconciling spirit toward those whom society scorns and rebukes.

Keep us from submitting to temptation. Perfect our faith and help us withstand Satan's lure. When we come asking, continue to receive us; when we seek guidance, help us to find your Spirit; as we knock at the door of your eternal dominion, help us to hear Jesus responding: Come, enter in!

ELEVENTH SUNDAY AFTER PENTECOST

Lectionary Readings for the Day
Ps. 28; II Kings 13:14–20a

Col. 3:1–11; Luke 12:13–21

Seasonal Color:

Green

The ledger showed a healthy profit. So, the landowner thought that it would be well to build larger storerooms. More grain could be stored and time could be taken to eat, drink, and be merry. Ah, but what if the landowner died during this life of ease, whose then would the riches be? Jesus taught the multitude to seek their treasure through obeying God rather than coveting earthly possessions.

Call to Worship
LEADER: Hear the voice of my supplication, O God, as I cry to you for help, as I lift up my hands to your most holy sanctuary.

RESPONSE: You are our strength and shield, O God; in you our hearts trust; with our songs we give you thanks.

LEADER: Let us worship God.

Prayer of Praise and Adoration
Great Shepherd of Israel, you hear the voices of our supplications; you defend your people as their strength and shield. Through Christ you have established our eternal birthright; by your Spirit you make us to know your godly decree. As we dwell evermore in the fold of your heavenly heritage, we blend our voices with the multitudes and sing praise to you.

Litany of Confession
LEADER: If then you have been raised with Christ, set your mind on things that are above.

RESPONSE: For you have died, and your life is hid with Christ in God.

LEADER: Put to death therefore what is earthly in you: fornication, impurity, passion, evil desire, and covetousness, which is idolatry.

RESPONSE: For you have died, and your life is hid with Christ in God.

LEADER: But now put them all away: anger, wrath, malice, slander, and foul talk from your mouth.

RESPONSE: For you have died, and your life is hid with Christ in God.
LEADER: Do not lie to one another, seeing that you have put off the old nature with its practices and have put on the new nature.
RESPONSE: For you have died, and your life is hid with Christ in God.

Prayer of Dedication

Our Shield and Defender, you have taught us how to trust your goodness and lay up treasure in heaven; we offer you gifts in response to your word. We bring you a portion of what our labor has gained in thankful praise for the abundance we have. We give you our souls in humble obedience, for in Christ we inherit eternal life. Be pleased with our offerings; they are signs of your mercy.

Prayer of Thanksgiving and Supplication

O God, our Rock and Redeemer, and solace for all who call on your name, we behold the vision of your holy splendor and bow down before you in humble submission. You are God; there is no other; all else fades and withers, while you endure throughout the ages. With angels, archangels, and prophets, apostles, and martyrs who have gone before, we join in giving you praise and thanksgiving.

Your grace abounds; we receive of its abundance; you exceed our expectations and needs. There is never a day that we cannot list the manifold gifts of your abounding love. From morning until nightfall, we are upheld by encompassing care.

Having been raised by Christ, we will set our minds on your heavenly splendor. We will trust your Holy Spirit to guide us when earthly desires distract us. We confess that we are prone to temptation, but by your grace we can put on the new nature Christ bestows.

Claiming our inheritance as your sons and daughters, we shall go forth to all people as witnesses to your love. Let us not covet what our neighbors enjoy. Prevent our worship of false gods, and stop our tongues when we would slander a sister or brother. When we eat, make us mindful that you are the source of all nourishment; when we drink, may it be the cup of new life. Help us to be merry in the joy of the Spirit, for then we shall give you the glory and honor you are due.

TWELFTH SUNDAY AFTER PENTECOST

Lectionary Readings for the Day

Ps. 14; Jer. 18:1–11

Heb. 11:1–3, 8–19; Luke 12:32–40

Seasonal Color:
Green

Discipleship is costly, but it is not to be fraught with anxiety. God is to be trusted for all one's needs. With their treasure in heaven they will not be afraid to give alms, for thieves cannot threaten their true possessions. Disciples free themselves of earthly care so they can wait and watch, for they do not know when the call will come.

Call to Worship

LEADER: The fool says, "There is no God." They are corrupt, and do abominable deeds, there is none that does good.

RESPONSE: God looks down from heaven upon us, to see if there are any who act wisely, who seek after God.

LEADER: Let us worship God.

Prayer of Praise and Adoration

O God in heaven, like a potter you framed the universe, and with your hands you made us. You fashioned creation to fulfill your purpose. Through Christ you restore that which is broken; by your Holy Spirit you enflame us with zeal to obey. Look down from heaven to see if there are any who act wisely; you will see us and hear us praising your name.

Prayer of Confession

UNISON: By faith you called Abraham to sojourn, O God; by faith Sarah conceived even when she was past the age. We read of their witness and marvel at their obedience; our faith is meager by comparison. We rarely venture out without knowing the destination; we want to know what's in it for us before we say yes to your call. Forgive our lack of daring and commitment and help us to trust you fully.

Assurance of Pardon

LEADER: Remember that "faith is the assurance of things hoped for, the conviction of things not seen. . . . By faith we understand that the world was created by the word of God, so that what is seen was made out of things which do not appear." We can, therefore, look "forward to the city which has foundations, whose builder and maker is God," for by the faith of Jesus the Christ we are forgiven.

Prayer of Dedication

Righteous God, you cast out fear and open the doors to your dominion; we come bearing alms, as Christ would have us do. All that we own you have given us. We set it apart to your glory and honor. Who we are is due to your graciousness; we commit our efforts to your service. Possess us and guide us through your Holy Spirit and we shall live out our days praising your name.

Prayer of Thanksgiving and Supplication

God of wisdom, righteousness, and grace, we are overcome by the benefits you have bestowed upon us. We need not fear, since in Christ you endow us with eternal life; you craft our talents and implant them within us; we live by your grace. Dying to sin and rising in the victory of Christ's atoning sacrifice, we can walk upright, thanks to your love.

Keep the lamp of your goodness burning brightly within us, as a sign of our welcome when Christ comes and knocks. If the candle of faith has grown dim and no longer leads us to obedience, trim our wick and ignite us anew. Doubt and depression make our worship halfhearted; startle us with your grace so that we regain the sense of wonder. When our confession becomes casual and we have little intention of changing our ways, call us to account by your righteousness and purify our motives.

As Abraham stepped out with assurance, not knowing where he was to go, may we likewise venture forth by the light of your promise. Deliver us from the excessive need to control our own destinies, and restore our trust in your infinite goodness. By your power Sarah conceived, even when she was past the age. Help us to bear within us the hope that in Christ all things are possible. With faith rekindled, we set forth on our journey in the certain knowledge that we are ever at home with you.

THIRTEENTH SUNDAY AFTER PENTECOST

Lectionary Readings for the Day
Ps. 10:12–18; Jer. 20:7–13

Heb. 12:1–2, 12–17; Luke 12:49–56

Seasonal Color:
Green

The fire of judgment and the water of baptism were symbols of Jesus' compelling call to ministry; they still are. What one enflames, the other can quench. Jesus forecasts a time of division when households will be divided. Within the household of faith, baptism is the sacrament that binds us together; whatever our differences, we are still one. As the body of Christ, obey what Christ teaches and be reconciled one to another.

Call to Worship
LEADER: Therefore, since we are surrounded by so great a cloud of witnesses, let us run with perseverance the race set before us,

RESPONSE: Looking to Jesus the pioneer and perfecter of our faith, who is seated at the right hand of the throne of God.

LEADER: Let us worship God.

Prayer of Praise and Adoration
You lift our drooping hands, O God, and strengthen our weak knees. You make straight the ways of the faithful and keep those who trust you from falling. We shall make known your holiness among the nations and proclaim your peace unto the ends of the earth. In the name of Jesus, who sits at your right hand, we gather to praise you, God of all grace.

Prayer of Confession
UNISON: Have mercy upon us, O God, for sin clings so closely and its burden is great. Because of sin, our hands are at our sides when they should reach out to others; our knees are shaky when we should be standing firm. We are victims of our own misdeeds; we cannot escape sin's weight on our lives. Through Christ's intercession lift the burden from us, and help us walk in freedom and in strength.

Assurance of Pardon
LEADER: Know that God is gracious and just, and forgives all who repent and turn from their sin. So run with perseverance the

race that is set, looking to Jesus the pioneer and perfecter of your faith. Because Christ sits at God's right hand and intercedes for us, we have assurance that we are forgiven.

Prayer of Dedication

All praise and honor be unto you, O God, for your faithfulness throughout the ages. We could offer you nothing were it not for Christ our Redeemer. We could not walk obediently without your Holy Spirit to guide us. We could not bring you our offerings except for your grace. We are yours, blessed God. Use us, now.

Prayer of Thanksgiving and Intercession

God of all knowledge, before whom nations rise and pass away, we bow down in awe of your infinite wisdom. You discern our inmost thoughts, sensing our needs. You are the quickening fire of judgment that renders us liable for our deeds and misdeeds. Yours is the reconciling Spirit of atonement, which can lift us from the depths of sin and failure. You set us aright, so that we may walk henceforth in your mercy; for all this and more we give you thanks.

God of compassion, we pray for those whose spirits are crushed by the weight of their afflictions. They cry in their anguish that there can be no God. Draw near to them during their time of trial, and deliver them from the abyss of despair. Help us be for them a source of encouragement and support, so that they may once more trust your promises. Let us hear in their cries our own call to be by their side.

God of justice, we pray for the doers of evil whose arms smite the weak and the powerful alike. They make no distinctions in their quest for power; they acknowledge no God who can requite their sin. When they are called to account before your throne, may Christ intercede on their behalf. Keep us from casting them aside as worthy only of punishment; teach us our dependence with them on your mercy. Help us, O God, to pray for both the oppressed and the oppressors, to the end that all may one day be included in your gift of redemption.

FOURTEENTH SUNDAY AFTER PENTECOST

Lectionary Readings for the Day
Ps. 84; Jer. 28:1–9
Heb. 12:18–29; Luke 13:22–30

Seasonal Color:
Green

After the householder has shut the door, many will seek entry and not gain it. There will be weeping and gnashing of teeth. Claims of past relationship with Jesus will not suffice, for some who are last will be first, and some who are first will be last. Enter by the narrow door and seek now your place at God's table, for people will come from east and west and from north and south to dine in God's eternal presence.

Call to Worship
LEADER: How lovely is your dwelling place, O God! My soul longs for your courts; my heart and flesh sing for joy.
RESPONSE: Even the sparrow finds a home, and the swallow a nest. Blessed are those who dwell in your house, ever singing your praise!
LEADER: Let us worship God.

Prayer of Praise and Adoration
Blessed are those whose strength is in you, O God of hosts, in whose hearts are highways to your eternal dominion. A day in your courts is better than a thousand elsewhere, and you withhold nothing from those who walk uprightly. We shall dwell as doorkeepers in your heavenly household, there to give you the honor and glory that is due your name.

Prayer of Confession
UNISON: With Christ as our hope, O God, we stand at the gates of your sanctuary seeking pardon. We confess that we have not worshiped you alone. Life makes its demands and we push you to the margins. You are for leisure moments, when our own work is done. Forgive us for our small minds and mistaken priorities. Restore in us the sense of your greatness and your ultimate claim upon our lives.

Assurance of Pardon
LEADER: Hear with grateful hearts that Jesus, the mediator of the new covenant, ushers us into the gates of God's eternal dominion. By his own blood he healed the estrangement between

us and God, and by his sacrifice offers reconciliation to all who believe. In this Christ we have assurance that we are forgiven, and truly citizens of the heavenly city.

Prayer of Dedication

With praise and adoration we enter your temple; thanksgiving spills from our lips as we approach your majesty. You are God who creates in splendor; holy and blessed is your glorious name. With your Spirit to guide us we shall strive to enter the narrow door, following Christ's teachings and the call to obey. Receive now these offerings as signs of our commitment, of our unceasing gratitude for the gifts you bestow.

Prayer of Thanksgiving and Supplication

How lovely is your dwelling place, O God of hosts. How spacious are the courts of your realm. Birds can come and build their nests; people can gather and find room at your table. Through Christ you have opened the gates to your heavenly Jerusalem, where we may enter in and taste the joys of salvation.

We thank you for the company of angels who teach us how to sing your praises. Make our life's journey a pilgrimage of praise and thanksgiving for the beauty, order, and worth you bestow on all of its parts. Keep us from taking our trek for granted, and from the misguided notion that whatever we do now affects not the whole.

We praise you for the firstborn already enrolled in heavenly splendor, prophets, priests, poets, and parents of our faith. Their visions of peace call us to greater endeavor. Their prayers on our behalf sustain us when our own words are found wanting, and their example abides with us still.

We rejoice at these tokens of your mercy, and are continually grateful for the gift of your Spirit. The Spirit strengthens us when temptation comes, and helps us to discern your will as we respond to the needs of our neighbors. Make us open channels of your love and clear signs to those who seek their way to you, to the end that all flesh may one day sing for joy.

FIFTEENTH SUNDAY AFTER PENTECOST

Lectionary Readings for the Day
Ps. 15; Ezek. 18:1–9, 25–29   *Seasonal Color:*
Heb. 13:1–8; Luke 14:1, 7–14   *Green*

House rules are the theme of today's readings—that is, how to govern ourselves in the household of faith. For example, sit at table in the lowest place; you may be invited to move up higher. When you give a party, invite those whom others might shun; you will be blessed. Two lessons are worth remembering: Be humble, and forget not the needy. God will exalt you and remember your faithfulness.

Call to Worship
LEADER: O God, who has the right to enter your tabernacle? Who may dwell on your holy mountain?
RESPONSE: Whoever walks blamelessly, does what is right, speaks the truth, and honors all who fear God shall never be moved.
LEADER: Let us worship God.

Prayer of Praise and Adoration
O God of truth and justice, in Christ you have taught what it means to obey you; we glorify your name. You are the immovable rock of salvation, the stone upon which we build our faith. When trials beset us, you offer safe haven; amid tribulation, you remain a bulwark of strength. We shall dwell all our days atop your holy mountain, and there offer glad praises for the salvation you bring.

Prayer of Confession
UNISON: Eternal Judge, cleanse our hearts of any ill will we may hold against neighbors. When they do not think as we do, we often judge them unenlightened. If they behave differently, we pin labels on them. We choose as our guests those we deem worthy of places of honor within our households. Yet through Christ you opened heaven to all without regard to their status in society. Forgive our inability to do the same, and save us from all pride and prejudice in our dealings with your children.

Assurance of Pardon
LEADER: Sisters and brothers, recall the words of Scripture. "Jesus Christ is the same yesterday and today and for ever." It is

Christ who said, "I will never fail you nor forsake you." So, come to Christ and there find assurance that in confessing our sin, we are forgiven.

Prayer of Dedication

God the heavenly host, you invite us to dine at your table. You anoint us through Christ with the oil of righteousness. Our cup overflows with the gift of the Holy Spirit. We come to your banquet of eternal redemption with gifts befitting our new life in Jesus. Receive them as signs of our commitment to be your faithful stewards.

Prayer of Thanksgiving

Heavenly Teacher, your word is everlasting; by it we are instructed. It shines like a beacon, guiding our way. Throughout the ages your word has led your people along paths of righteousness; by it the wicked have turned from their evil deeds, and those who suffer have found havens of comfort. The neglected have felt its soothing balm, and those seeking salvation have found their way to your promised deliverance.

We give thanks for Jesus, the Word made flesh. He taught what it meant to obey you completely. He lives today in the pages of Scripture, and in our hearts. Through him we hear your proclamation of freedom from all that binds us. His word is alive in the waters of our baptism, cleansing us and clothing us in the garments of new life. He is alive as host of the heavenly banquet where all may gather and partake of the bread of reconciliation and the cup of salvation.

We praise you for the Holy Spirit, who guides us safely through every trial and tribulation. When valleys are deep and we despair of finding sure exit, the Spirit protects us and grants us clear passage. When we are captive to our creaturely comforts, the Spirit goads us to take that first step of faith. We shall seek to walk blamelessly in such counsel and wisdom; we shall speak the truth implanted once and for all by Jesus the Christ.

SIXTEENTH SUNDAY AFTER PENTECOST

Lectionary Readings for the Day
Ps. 94:12–22; Ezek. 33:1–11   *Seasonal Color:*
Philemon 1–20; Luke 14:25–33   *Green*

The subject is, again, the cost of discipleship. At what expense does one follow the Christ? It is well to consider the consequences before embarking on any major venture. Some forsake family and friendships in order to be faithful disciples; any who cannot carry the cross ought to rethink their decision. To follow Christ involves renouncing allegiance to whoever and whatever may get in the way. Are you ready?

Call to Worship
LEADER: O God, you forsake not your people, nor abandon your heritage; justice will return to the righteous, for the upright to follow.
RESPONSE: You have become my stronghold, O God, the rock of my refuge. When my foot slips, you will uphold me.
LEADER: Let us worship God.

Prayer of Praise and Adoration
O God, our Rock and Redeemer, you are the stronghold and the refuge of faith, the foundation of hope, and the safeguard for all who praise your name. With you we can walk and not stumble, run and not fall, and lie down in safety. We shall fill our days with visions of your lofty splendor, and consider each moment as sacred because of your grace.

Prayer of Confession
UNISON: God in Christ, who endured the cross in your own flesh for our sakes, hear us as we confess our sin. We would be your bold disciples, but we fear suffering; we would carry our cross, but it weighs too heavily. We count the cost of following you— as long as there are benefits; but to renounce all we have is a devastating prospect. Forgive the conditions we make when we try to obey, and free us by your grace to forsake all and follow you.

Assurance of Pardon

LEADER: God is just and takes no pleasure in the death of the wicked. Through Christ there is hope of eternal forgiveness. Turn back from your past and embrace God's promised assurance: In Christ there is redemption and release from all sin.

Prayer of Dedication

God of grace and peace, we come as free agents of Christ's reconciling love. We give our lives as a thank offering for the bountiful mercies you bestow on us. You refresh our hearts by the gift of a savior; may what we bring enrich others who seek your deliverance. Take us and use us as stewards of your grace and peace.

Prayer of Thanksgiving and Supplication

O God of freedom and justice, who alone can break the fetters of bondage which enslave us, we give you thanks that in Jesus we can walk freely as your sons and daughters. While we were slaves to sin, he rescued us. To us who were caught in the trap of self-deception, he showed your mercy. Yea, he himself endured death so that we might live eternally. It is through him that we can approach you in prayer.

Hear us as we offer our petitions and seek your grace to embark once more on faith's journey. Through your Holy Spirit continue to endow us with the wisdom befitting our high calling. When we are tempted to forsake you and live to ourselves, keep us from yielding to such vain notions. Help us rather to honor the yearning within to please you and be worthy of your trust.

Guide us in our quest for Christ's liberating righteousness, the keys that unlock whatever keeps our neighbors imprisoned. If it is disease, help us to give what we can for further research. If it is poverty, give us boldness to attack the systems of oppression and greed. If it is bigotry, purify us from our prejudice and enable us to proclaim Christ's reconciling atonement.

We pray for those who have not yet tasted the sweet fruits of freedom. Make us ever conscious of their plight. As Christ suffered for our sakes, make us willing to bear the cross on their behalf. As Christ rose victoriously, help us to demonstrate the risen life through acts of liberation from bondage. As Christ welcomes all to dine at your table, prepare us for the day when, united, we can feast on your grace.

SEVENTEENTH SUNDAY AFTER PENTECOST

Lectionary Readings for the Day

Ps. 77:11–20; Hos. 4:1–3; 5:15 to 6:6   *Seasonal Color:*
I Tim. 1:12–17; Luke 15:1–10   *Green*

To find what was lost is cause for rejoicing, even though the search seemed endless. What is lost preoccupies our thinking; we retrace our steps in search of some clues. God's quest is consuming in search of lost ones. There is rejoicing in heaven when someone repents.

Call to Worship

LEADER: I will call to mind your deeds, O God; yea, I will remember your wonders of old.
RESPONSE: I will meditate on your work and muse on your deeds. Your way is holy; there is no god so great.
LEADER: Let us worship God.

Prayer of Praise and Adoration

Great and wonderful are all your works, O God; majestic is your name. Unto the ends of the earth you display your dominion; beyond the reaches of the heavens your glory shines. Hear the praises we offer as we gather to worship; receive the confession we make through your mercy and grace. As we open your Word, we discern your goodness. Your way is holy, great God of all.

Prayer of Confession

UNISON: Praise be unto you, God of mercy and might, and to your only-begotten, our Savior Christ Jesus. In spite of our sin, Christ calls us to ministry. Christ is patient and loving, reflecting your nature. We dishonor your name and persecute our neighbors; we are not deserving of the trust you place in us. We confess our wrongdoing and plead your forgiveness; through Christ accept us and cleanse us of all sin.

Assurance of Pardon

LEADER: "The saying is sure and worthy of acceptance, that Christ Jesus came into the world to save sinners." By Christ's mercy we have been born anew into a life of hope, becoming, for those who would follow, an example of God's patience and trust.

To the God of ages, "immortal, invisible, the only God, be honor and glory for ever and ever." Amen.

Prayer of Dedication

O God, you desire steadfast love and not sacrifice; we seek to know you, not to placate you. We offer ourselves, and what we have. Accept our gifts as signs of our commitment to love you more fully, and receive our response in obedience as a symbol of our dedication to serve.

Prayer of Thanksgiving and Supplication

Great and wonderful are your works, O God; they are awesome to behold and worthy to be praised. You are a shepherd who cannot rest until all the sheep are safely gathered. You are the keeper of fine treasure who searches for even one coin until it is found. You are the God who sent Jesus to redeem a lost and fallen humanity. He bore our sins and paid the cost of our guilt.

Give us, we pray, a measure of your patience as we seek the wandering. Keep us from hastily disregarding their plight. Some are lost because they have been misguided; help us to show them the proper way. Others choose to march to the beat of their own drummer. Give us ears to hear their source of enlightenment, and the boldness to share with them our faith in Christ. Uphold by your Spirit those who truly seek to repent of their past and start anew. May they be borne on Christ's shoulders to a homecoming within the confines of your beloved community.

We give thanks for the treasures stored within each of us. Keep them from becoming tarnished by neglect or abuse. As in Christ you have made us worthy of your grace, may all that we do radiate your blessing and glory. If it is to proclaim the good news of Christ, make our words clear and convincing. If it is to heal, teach us to be as consoling to others as Christ is compassionate with us. If it is voluntary service, show us the mind of Christ, who gave without thought of return. Amen.

EIGHTEENTH SUNDAY AFTER PENTECOST

Lectionary Readings for the Day

Ps. 107:1–9; Hos. 11:1–11   *Seasonal Color:*
I Tim. 2:1–7; Luke 16:1–13   *Green*

The lesson is clear: no one can serve two masters. If we treasure riches, then we are tempted to pile up as much as possible. If we treasure God, then all that we have is committed to the service of God. We must decide whom we will serve. There is no halfway ground.

Call to Worship

LEADER: Give thanks to God, for God is good; God's steadfast love endures for ever!

RESPONSE: All nations shall thank you, O God, for your wonderful works. You satisfy the thirsty, and the hungry you fill.

LEADER: Let us worship God.

Prayer of Praise and Adoration

Giver of every good and perfect gift, your steadfast love endures forever. You redeem the nations from distress and trouble; you gather your people from the corners of the earth. We enter your courts singing thanksgiving for the bountiful mercies you lavish upon us. Hear our glad praises and be pleased with our worship, for you are worthy of all honor.

Prayer of Confession

UNISON: Merciful God, you lead us by the cords of compassion; we seek your forgiveness through Christ's intercession. Fill us anew with your Holy Spirit, so that we may faithfully obey your will. When we are vengeful, purge our thoughts of resentment and anger. When we bear false witness, turn us from deceit to truthfulness. Cleanse us of selfish desires, and free us to respond to your holy word. In righteousness remake us, and through Christ restore us.

Assurance of Pardon

LEADER: God our Savior desires that all should be saved and come to the knowledge of truth. There is one God, and one mediator, Christ Jesus, who came as a ransom for all. With assurance and conviction I say to you: God in Christ forgives us our sin.

Prayer of Dedication

Redeemed by Christ and gathered to praise you, we come with thanksgiving, O God our Savior. You relieve our hunger and quench our thirst; you fill us with good things and satisfy our needs. How shall we respond to such goodness and mercy? By committing all that we have to your honor and glory. Accept our offerings and receive our tributes, for they belong to you.

Prayer of Petition and Supplication

God our Savior, to lift our prayers to you is good and acceptable. Hear us now as we come before you. Christ dwells by your side to intercede for us when our words fail. Angel songs blend with our voices, filling the air with hymns of praise. You are clothed with all honor and majesty. You alone are God and we adore you.

Hear us as we pray for those to whom we have entrusted the authority of government. We pray for their health, that they may be able to withstand the pressures of office. We pray for those who advise them, that they may be given the wisdom required for each circumstance. We pray for the families, loved ones, and friends of our leaders, that they may be supportive in the midst of the burdens of public life.

Hear us as we pray for ourselves as citizens. Help us to be responsible and to blend the diversity of opinions into unified concern for the well-being of all. Deliver us from suspicions of one another, and help us to focus rather on the good of all. Save us from becoming high and mighty, and lead us in the paths of service.

You have taught us through Christ that we can serve only one. We commit our allegiance to you alone. May all that we do be to your glory, so that one day we may hear your, "Well done, good and faithful servant."

NINETEENTH SUNDAY AFTER PENTECOST

Lectionary Readings for the Day

Ps. 107:1, 33–43; Joel 2:23–30   *Seasonal Color:*
I Tim. 6:6–19; Luke 16:19–31   *Green*

The lesson of Scripture is plain: riches blind us to the will of God and lead to temptations that destroy. The call to justice lies at the mansion gate, but we fail to show mercy to the homeless. The consequences of such neglect are eternal. Christ calls us now to hear and to repent. Those in the grip of famine cannot wait.

Call to Worship

LEADER: Give thanks to God, for God is good; God's steadfast love endures for ever!
RESPONSE: Let whoever is wise take heed of God's goodness; let all consider God's steadfast love.
LEADER: Let us worship God.

Prayer of Praise and Adoration

Your goodness goes before us, O Holy Redeemer, and the upright rejoice in your radiant splendor. Your touch turns deserts into pools of living water; as you embrace the land, its yield abounds. With wisdom you implant, we shall proclaim your virtue; through our Savior Christ Jesus we shall sing your praise without ceasing.

Prayer of Confession

UNISON: God of grace, we stand in need of your forgiveness. Desiring to be rich, we fall into temptation. Love of money ensnares us. Enough does not satisfy: the more we acquire, the greater our greed becomes. We become prosperous in our own eyes, and poor in your sight. Rescue us from self-destruction through Christ, the giver of life.

Assurance of Pardon

LEADER: Sisters and brothers, fight the good fight of faith; aim at righteousness, godliness, love, and gentleness; take hold of the eternal life to which you were called when you made the good confession in the presence of many witnesses. And Christ, who alone can keep you from falling, will deliver you blameless before the throne of God. In Christ, we are forgiven.

Prayer of Dedication

Merciful Provider, all that we have is a gift of your goodness; whatever we acquire we gain by your grace. You cause the rains to yield abundant harvests; you send the sun to nourish rich growth. We bring you gifts wrought by your handiwork and dedicate our lives to tending your creation. Accept us as stewards within your dominion, and bless all our efforts on your behalf.

Prayer of Thanksgiving and Supplication

God of heaven, where angels dwell, we give thanks for Christ, in whom we glimpse your eternal realm. Through Christ you have poured out your Spirit upon all of your children; those who believe see visions of your splendor and dream dreams of your glory. We praise you that we are numbered among those who can climb Calvary's hill and behold the heavens opening to reveal your majesty.

We are grateful for Christ's mediation as we make our confession; he intercedes for us when our words are found wanting and our actions fall short of your will for us. We would aim at righteousness, but greed devours us; we yearn for riches with consuming desire. Teach us again how you clothe and feed creation, and help us to trust in your design for our lives.

We would be loving, but hostility hinders us. We are suspicious of our neighbors and begrudge them their due. As Christ bore the cross in spite of our sinfulness, make us more sympathetic to our neighbor's burdens. As you raised Christ on the third day and robbed death of its victory, raise us to renewed acts of compassion, so that sisters and brothers can see what it means to be free.

Teach us, O God, what it costs to obey. Send forth your Spirit to counsel and guide us. As we embark on faith's journey, keep us free from reproach. We look to the day when Christ shall come, and pray that we may be found ready.

TWENTIETH SUNDAY AFTER PENTECOST

Lectionary Readings for the Day
Ps. 101; Amos 5:6–7, 10–15
II Tim. 1:1–14; Luke 17:5–10

Seasonal Color:
Green

Relationship with God implies obedience, duties to be fulfilled in grateful response to what God has done. To be a servant of Christ is a high calling. Christ called the disciples and empowered them; they were to serve in Christ's name and give God the glory. Think of your discipleship as a mandate to be faithful; it is a gift you have received, not an honor you have won.

Call to Worship
LEADER: Seek good, and not evil, that you may live; and so the God of hosts will be with you, as you have said.
RESPONSE: I will sing of loyalty and justice, O God; and give heed to the way that is blameless. Come, dwell with us!
LEADER: Let us worship God.

Prayer of Praise and Adoration
We shall dwell in your house forever, O God, and seek to live upright and blameless lives in Christ Jesus, our guide. You show us your mercy; Christ teaches us justice; we live by your Spirit, who enlightens our way. Blessed Trinity, you do not forsake us; we can walk with integrity because of your love. Hear our glad praises as we enter your sanctuary; you are worthy of all glory your children can bring.

Prayer of Confession
UNISON: O God, who by your Spirit can rekindle the embers of faith, purge us of all sin and make of us obedient servants. We are guilty of pushing you to life's periphery; we serve you only when it seems convenient. We follow the Christ when it is to our benefit; we call on the Spirit when our own efforts fail. Remake us in your image of righteousness, and teach us the meaning of discipleship.

Assurance of Pardon
LEADER: "Do not be ashamed then of testifying to God, . . . who saved us and called us with a holy calling, not in virtue of our works but in virtue of God's own purpose and the grace God gave

us in Christ Jesus years ago." By that grace we are saved as through Christ we are forgiven.

Prayer of Dedication

We sing of your loyalty and justice, O God; we tell of your handiwork to all generations. You call us to faithfulness; therefore we shall seek to be blameless in all that we do. Accept our commitment to ministry as your Spirit guides us, and be pleased with the offerings we bring. Make us useful within the gates of your righteousness, so that justice shall reign throughout the land.

Prayer of Thanksgiving

God of grace, mercy, and peace, we thank you for the ministry to which you call us, the teaching which guides us, and the intercession of Christ when we stumble and fall. We are mindful of his suffering for our sakes, and grateful for his victory over evil. No longer can the powers of death claim absolute control over us, for we are Christ's and he is victor over death.

We thank you for the Spirit who nurtures us toward our first steps in faith. The Spirit keeps us from falling, and plants our feet on the rock which none can move. By the Spirit we can see beyond today and catch a glimpse of a new heaven and a new earth.

With your Spirit to guide and Christ to intercede for us, we venture forth with confidence on our pilgrimage. We give thanks for ancestors in faith whose example we may follow; we stand on their shoulders and view the heavenly city. Their stories are a rich legacy of insight; they faced the abyss and remained steadfast. Their testimony is etched forever on the hearts of your people, O God. Send us forth in their spirit and make us worthy of generations to come.

TWENTY-FIRST SUNDAY AFTER PENTECOST

Lectionary Readings for the Day
Ps. 26; Micah 1:2; 2:1–10
II Tim. 2:8–15; Luke 17:11–19

Seasonal Color:
Green

Ten lepers begged Jesus for mercy. Jesus sent them to the priests and as they went they were cleansed. But only one, an outsider at that, returned to praise God for the healing received. "Where are the nine?" asked Jesus. The lesson is this: Have faith that your prayer will be answered, and in faith thank God for the mercy you received.

Call to Worship
LEADER: O God, I love the habitation of your house, and the place where your glory dwells.
RESPONSE: My foot stands on level ground; in the great congregation I will bless you, O God.
LEADER: Let us worship God.

Prayer of Praise and Adoration
We come within the gates of your heavenly dominion and enter your courts to give you our praise. You are God whose splendor fills all the temple; our eyes behold the signs of your steadfast love. With our hands cleansed through the forgiveness of Jesus we shall go about your altar singing songs of thanksgiving. Your works are wondrous and worthy of tribute; hear our rejoicing as we lift before you glad adoration.

Prayer of Confession
UNISON: In the name of Christ Jesus, descended from David and risen in glory, we make our confession. Disputes arise within congregations; brothers and sisters quarrel. Hostility fractures the body; conflict leads to suspicion and pain. Forgive us, O God, when we continue to bear grudges; reconcile us to our neighbor as you redeem us of sin.

Assurance of Pardon
LEADER: "The saying is sure: If we have died with Christ, we shall also live with Christ; if we endure, we shall also reign with Christ. . . . Do your best to present yourself to God as one approved, . . . rightly handling the word of truth." The truth is this: In Christ we are forgiven.

Prayer of Dedication

God of goodness, you bind up the wounds of the afflicted; we come with thanksgiving for your boundless acts of mercy. Receive now our offerings; use them to heal the suffering, to shelter the homeless, to comfort the lonely, and to make whole once again those whose lives are broken. We give what we have in the name of Christ, who gave to all who believe the gift of hope.

Prayer of Thanksgiving and Supplication

O God, whose name is worthy of unending praise, we bow before you in humble submission. Words fail to communicate our depth of love to you and our yearning to obey your will. Without your Spirit day follows day in aimless succession. Nothing can compare with the love you have shown us, not the tribute of leaders, the fame of achievement, the applause of friends and loved ones. We owe all to your mercy; we will praise you at all times and call upon your name.

Hear us as we pray for cleansing; rid us of the vanity which clutters our thinking. Show us the Christ who taught self-denial. Help us to hear once again how the humble received mercy, the sick were healed, and those whom good people rejected were loved and forgiven.

Increase our faith and save us from the need to boast of our own goodness. As we are quick to call on you for guidance when we are threatened, let us be as eager to give you the glory for whatever we gain. Fill us anew with your Holy Spirit, so that our words may be your words, our work your work, and our glory your glory. You are the God of our salvation to whom belongs all glory, praise, and honor, now and forevermore.

TWENTY-SECOND SUNDAY AFTER PENTECOST

Lectionary Readings for the Day
Ps. 119:137–144; Hab. 1:1–3; 2:1–4
II Tim. 3:14 to 4:5; Luke 18:1–8

Seasonal Color:
Green

The widow was wearing out the poor judge! By his own admission he cared little about God or people, but what was he to do with this persistent woman? The Gospel tells us that he finally vindicated her, just to get her "off his back." If a judge like this will vindicate a plaintiff, God will surely vindicate the elect who cry for justice.

Call to Worship
LEADER: O God, you are righteous and right are your judgments. Your instruction is just; it is fixed firm and sure.

RESPONSE: Your justice is everlasting and your law is truth. Give me understanding that I may live.

LEADER: Let us worship God.

Prayer of Praise and Adoration
Righteous One of all generations, how glorious is your name. You speak and worlds are created; you establish the boundaries of the seas and the land. Your countenance illumines the heavens above us; your righteousness is known throughout all the earth. We live by your mercy and depend on your blessings; we give you all praise.

Prayer of Confession
UNISON: O God, our Judge and Redeemer, we confess that we have failed in our ministry to others. We listen for teachings to our own liking; we yearn for doctrines that boost our egos. We follow those who flatter us; we seek comfort and not challenge from our confessions of faith. Renew a right spirit within us, O God, and train us in righteousness as you forgive our sin.

Assurance of Pardon
LEADER: Sisters and brothers, "continue in what you have learned and firmly believed, knowing from whom you learned it and how from childhood you have been acquainted with the sacred writings which are able to instruct you for salvation

through faith in Christ Jesus." For the truth of the gospel abides: In Jesus Christ, we are forgiven.

Prayer of Dedication

Source of all goodness, power, and strength, we come with gifts in response to your love. You pour out your goodness; we bring you thanksgiving. You infuse us with power; we offer the fruits of our labor. You sustain us with strength; all that we do we dedicate to your glory. Honor us and bless those endeavors, which are a testimony to your abiding grace.

Prayer of Thanksgiving and Supplication

Righteous Judge, you temper judgment with mercy; we praise and thank you for your loving-kindness. Though we are not worthy even to eat the crumbs from your table, you have set a place for us and invite us to dine. With Christ, the bread of life, we are continually nourished; through Christ, the living Word, you reveal your gracious will for our lives. In Christ, who lives and reigns to guide us, we pray without ceasing.

Open our eyes to new insight into what it means to be called your people. When destruction is all about us, hear our cries for direction and make us quick to respond. When your children cry out for refuge and safety, give us compassion to embrace them with care. When your people suffer from injustice and bondage, empower us in Christ's name to set them free. Place us in a tower as watchers over your creation, and grant us the vision of how the righteous shall live.

Give patience to endure and strength to withstand the trials that await. When we cannot rise above the movement of the masses, set our feet on higher ground and give us boldness to proclaim your will for all. When the cross weighs heavily and we strain to confront those who oppose your way, grant us sure faith and steady nerves to confess that you alone are God. From the vantage you give us may we become beacons of faith, hope, and love, to the end that all may know your goodness.

TWENTY-THIRD SUNDAY AFTER PENTECOST

:tionary Readings for the Day
Ps. 3; Zeph. 3:1–9
II Tim. 4:6–8, 16–18; Luke 18:9–14

Seasonal Color:
Green

How we pray says a lot about our understanding of God. Jesus told a story of two people at prayer: one was a Pharisee, the other a tax collector. The Pharisee thanked God that he was not as others—unjust, extortioners. The tax collector could only beat his breast and beg God for mercy. Jesus declared that the tax collector went away justified. Those who exalt themselves will be humbled, and those who humble themselves before God will be exalted.

⟶ Call to Worship

LEADER: O God, when my foes rise up against me, you are my shield and defender; in you I put my trust.

RESPONSE: When I lie down and sleep you protect me from evil; I awaken to the dawn of new life in Christ.

LEADER: Let us worship God. Deliverance belongs to God, your blessing be upon your people.

Prayer of Praise and Adoration

Shield and Defender, how worthy you are of the praises we bring. We sing of your mercy; we tell of your glory; we speak of your greatness to the assembled throng. We need only cry aloud and you will hear, O God; you send your Spirit as our comfort and strength. We shall dwell evermore within your enfolding protection through the faith of Christ Jesus, in whose name we pray.

Prayer of Confession

UNISON: To fear you is the beginning of wisdom, O God, and to confess our sins can lead to repentance. We acknowledge the wrongs we commit against neighbors, the remarks that aim at tearing them down, the actions that exclude, the subtle and not so subtle distinctions that "put them in their place." Forgive us for our love of comfort in a world that is hungry and thirsty, and help us to amend our ways, through the merit and intercession of Jesus Christ.

Assurance of Pardon

LEADER: Hear the good news: Christ delivers those who are truly sorry and repent of their sins. Christ intercedes on their behalf before the judgment seat of Almighty God. Christ cleanses them and makes them fit to dwell in God's heavenly dominion. In Jesus Christ we are forgiven.

Prayer of Dedication

Merciful God, teach us to trust you to supply all our needs. You are the source of manna in our wilderness wanderings, the giver of the bread of life along the pilgrimage of faith. We bring you our offering with praise and thanksgiving for your constant care and protection.

Prayer of Thanksgiving and Intercession

O God, who so loved the world that you came in human form to live among us, we give thanks that through Christ we can open our hearts to you. Your people praise you amid the canyons of city streets; you hear their cries from the valleys of death's shadow. You welcome the shouts of joy from the mountaintops; you stoop to listen to sighs from the squalor of peasant villages. Wherever your people dwell, you sense their needs and receive their praise.

As in Jerusalem of the prophets, so today there are conditions in our world that cry for justice. Cities are racially segregated, poverty abounds. People languish without hope for employment; frustration moves toward violent protest. There are homeless, exposed to the elements, passing through life's seasons with worn bodies and bowed heads. Neighbors prey on each other, trampling on the dignity with which you endowed all your children. We feel helpless to alter their lot.

We pray for all these, O God, and for ourselves, that we may become instruments of change in this world. Embolden us to hold public officials accountable for human welfare; make us wise in the ways of justice, so that laws are fair and fairly administered. Make us the threads of hope, which, when woven together by common endeavor, become the tapestry of a just society, through Christ, the giver of hope.

TWENTY-FOURTH SUNDAY AFTER PENTECOST

Lectionary Readings for the Day
Ps. 65:1–8; Hag. 2:1–9

II Thess. 1:5–12; Luke 19:1–10

Seasonal Color:
Green

Zacchaeus climbed a sycamore tree to get a better view. Jesus spotted him and said, "Come down; for I must stay at your house today." There was murmuring at this. Now Zacchaeus was a tax collector, and rich; he was also a sinner in the eyes of many. Jesus came to save sinners. Respectable people are always offended by this.

Call to Worship
LEADER: Praise is due to thee, O God, in Zion; and to thee shall vows be performed, O thou who hearest prayer!

RESPONSE: Blessed is the one whom thou dost choose and bring near. We shall be satisfied with the goodness of thy holy temple!

LEADER: Let us worship God.

Prayer of Praise and Adoration
O God of our salvation, with dread deeds you answer us with deliverance; you are the hope of all the ends of the earth and of the farthest seas. By your strength you establish the mountains and still the waters. You calm the troubled breasts of all who put their trust in you. We shall not cease to give you praise and bless your holy name.

Prayer of Confession
UNISON: Righteous God, who deem it just to repay with affliction those who mistreat your children, forgive the sins we commit which harm our neighbors. Temper your vengeance when we claim not to know you. Ease your wrath when we fail to obey the gospel Christ taught. Let the glory of your might undergird our endeavors, as through Christ you deliver us from our weakness and shame. O God, have mercy upon us and fill us with your splendor.

Assurance of Pardon
LEADER: "To this end we always pray for you, that our God may make you worthy of God's call, and may fulfil every good resolve

and work of faith by God's power, so that the name of Jesus may be glorified in you, and you in Christ, according to the grace of our God and our Savior Christ Jesus," in whose name we are forgiven.

Prayer of Dedication

Chosen to serve you, we bring you our tributes. You are the God who delivers us; glad praises we sing. All that we have are gifts of your graciousness. You plumb our potential, our yield increases; we are stewards of your mercy, called to serve. Accept these offerings as signs of our faithfulness throughout each day.

Prayer of Thanksgiving and Supplication

Host of heaven, by whose gracious will Christ invites the household to dine, we give thanks that we are numbered among those who have places at your table. By your mercy you have broken the walls that divide us, uniting rich and poor, people of all shades, the lame and the spry, the bright and the bland, the loyal and the disloyal. All are reconciled by the One who broke bread that night so that our separations could be healed. We give thanks for the love displayed in that hospitable act.

Help us to climb with Zacchaeus above the press of the crowd and catch sight of Jesus, who came to make each person whole. Erase within us the tendency to blot out diversity, as if only those like us had anything to offer. Help us to see in all the stroke of your brush, the blending of hues, highlighting of shadows, harmonizing of subtleties, the rainbow of beauty your covenant foretold.

Make of this house a hospice where all find shelter, whose doors are opened when others are shut. Let there be no strangers here where Jesus is the host.

Send us forth with renewed commitment to seek out those whom society has abandoned. Make us quick to recognize their dignity, to affirm their right to self-determination, and to assist them in their quest for wholeness. Help us to welcome sinners as we have been welcomed by you, Christ Jesus.

TWENTY-FIFTH SUNDAY AFTER PENTECOST

Lectionary Readings for the Day
Ps. 9:11–20; Zech. 7:1–10

II Thess. 2:13 to 3:5; Luke 20:27–38

Seasonal Color:
Green

Human relationships here on earth have certain dynamics. At the resurrection a wholly different reality obtains. The Sadducees sought to relate the two orders; Jesus must answer that it cannot be done. In this age people marry and are given in marriage; in the age to come they neither marry nor are given in marriage. Whether now or in the age to come, God is God of the living, not God of the dead.

Call to Worship
LEADER: Sing praises to God, who dwells in Zion! Tell among the peoples God's deeds!

RESPONSE: Be gracious to me, O God, that I may recount all your praises and rejoice in your deliverance.

LEADER: Let us worship God.

Prayer of Praise and Adoration
You are worthy of all praise, O God; your judgment is sure. Like a refiner's fire, you purify your people and temper their desires. The heat is your love for them; the flame is the Spirit's power within; the light is the light which illumines the world. Come, fire from above, and fill our beings, as we worship and adore our maker.

Litany of Assurance
LEADER: Sisters and brothers, we are bound to give thanks to God always for you.

RESPONSE: God is faithful and will strengthen you and guard you from evil.

LEADER: God chose you from the beginning to be saved, through sanctification by the Spirit and belief in the truth.

RESPONSE: God is faithful and will strengthen you and guard you from evil.

LEADER: Sisters and brothers, stand firm and hold to the traditions which you were taught, whether by spoken or written word.

RESPONSE: God is faithful and will strengthen you and guard you from evil.

LEADER: Now may God, who loved us and gave us eternal comfort through grace, comfort your hearts in every good work and word.

RESPONSE: May the Savior direct your hearts to the love of God and to the steadfastness of Christ.

Prayer of Dedication

Gracious Comforter, we have sought to render true judgment, show kindness, accompany the sojourner, and devise no evil within our own hearts. May the tribute we render be worthy of the trust you place in us. Accept our offerings of praise and thanksgiving, as in Christ's name we pray.

Prayer of Thanksgiving and Supplication

Eternal God, from whom all goodness flows, we give thanks for Jesus Christ, who opens for us the gates to eternity. By your Holy Spirit lift us high above the cares that weigh upon us; let our spirits soar on the clouds of your merciful redemption, so that we may catch sight of your dominion and glory. Teach us your perfect will, and guide us in the path of righteousness; speak peace to our restless minds, that your ways may become our ways and Christ's call our fervent desire.

You are present everywhere, in countryside and city street, in family and in solitude. Be a sign for us as we seek to follow you. Help us to move beyond the convenient boundaries of our lives and touch the lives of others. Let us sing the glad song that Jesus has come to heal every human hurt.

Grant that we may live, move, and have our being in constant awareness of your grace and blessing. As we traverse the hours you give us daily, grace our footsteps, that they may follow those of Christ. When the sunlight fades and our bodies grow weary, let all we have been and done throughout the day serve as our prayer of thanks, through Christ our Savior.

TWENTY-SIXTH SUNDAY AFTER PENTECOST

Lectionary Readings for the Day

Ps. 82; Mal. 4:1–6   *Seasonal Color:*
II Thess. 3:6–13; Luke 21:5–19   *Green*

Jesus foresaw a time of distress and travail for his followers. Nation will rise against nation; there will be earthquakes, famine, terror, and signs from heaven. God's people will face persecution and be delivered to the authorities. Yet they are to endure and bear witness to the truth, for God will be with them.

Call to Worship

LEADER: It is God who rescues the weak and the needy and delivers them from the hand of the wicked.
RESPONSE: Arise, O God, judge the earth; for to you belong all the nations!
LEADER: Let us worship God.

Prayer of Praise and Adoration

God of righteousness, truth, and justice, who did judge your people according to the statutes delivered to Moses, we praise you for the mercy of Christ's intercession. In Christ's name we gather and are assured of your presence; we bow in adoration; we sing of your glory; your word is proclaimed for our guidance and nurture. Look now with favor on our worship, as in Christ we seek to be faithful.

Prayer of Confession

UNISON: God of consuming fire, treat us not as stubble through the folly of our misdeeds. We are misled by arrogance as we boast of our goodness; we look with disdain on those less fortunate, and ignore the poverty of our own souls. Claiming to be among the mighty, we favor those gifted with similar strengths. As individuals and as a nation, we test your patience. Yet in Christ you love us still. Forgive our pride and restore our sanity, so that we may yet serve you.

Assurance of Pardon

LEADER: Sisters and brothers, it is God who gives justice to the weak and maintains the right of the afflicted and destitute. God rescues the needy and delivers them from the hand of the wicked. As you confess your sins, God is faithful and just and will through Christ deliver you blameless in the day of God's judgment. In Jesus Christ we are forgiven.

Prayer of Dedication

Redeemer of the nations, great and wonderful are your works. All that we bring you have provided; only your grace renders our acts worthy of praise. Receive our tributes as praise and thanksgiving for your benevolent care, and multiply our efforts to your everlasting glory; for we offer our gifts in the name of Jesus Christ, the obedient one.

Prayer of Thanksgiving and Intercession

Judge of the universe, you know that we live in a great and awful time. You have opened our minds to the secrets of nature, placed in our hands the power of the atom, and allowed us to explore the heavens. Through human skill the earth yields an abundance of food; through the marvels of medicine our earthly span is extended beyond threescore and ten. We bow in humble thanksgiving and acknowledge your grace by which alone we survive.

As generations before us pled for your mercy, so we today entreat your goodness. We pray for modesty as we inhabit the earth's surface. Save us from destroying such a beautiful home. Endow our leaders with wisdom and a love of creation. Fill them with zeal for peace to match their obsession for defense. We pray for the success and safety of the modern explorers. Grant that their discoveries may increase for all people the gifts of your providential care. Help us to be more faithful stewards of the resources you provide. Replace greed with a gracious sharing of our abundance. We pray for the healers and those who preserve life. May longer lives bring a greater sense of your saving love.

As in Christ you came to show your love for the world, so through Christ we pray that the world you love may be saved for future generations.

TWENTY-SEVENTH SUNDAY AFTER PENTECOST
CHRIST THE KING

Lectionary Readings for the Day
Ps. 95; II Sam. 5:1–5

Col. 1:11–20; John 12:9–19

Seasonal Color:
White

The crowd went to see Jesus and Lazarus, whom Jesus had raised from the dead. What was the crowd seeking—a miracle worker, a ruler, healer, charismatic leader? Why do people seek Jesus today? Before answering the question, remember that God first sought you and sent Jesus into the world as living proof of God's love. Then seek Jesus, that you may, like Lazarus, have life eternal.

Call to Worship
LEADER: O come, let us sing unto God; let us make a noise to the rock of our salvation!

RESPONSE: Let us come into God's presence with thanksgiving; let us make a joyful noise with songs of praise!

LEADER: Let us worship God.

Prayer of Praise and Adoration
We come into your courts with praise, O God, and sing in glad adoration. You fill the temple with your majestic presence; we bow in awe at the sight of your holiness. Your goodness and mercy shall follow us all the days of our life, as in Christ we shall dwell in your house forever.

Litany of Assurance
LEADER: Give thanks to God, who has qualified us to share in the inheritance as enlightened saints.

RESPONSE: For in Christ all the fulness of God was pleased to dwell.

LEADER: God has delivered us from the dominion of darkness and in Christ we have redemption, the forgiveness of sins.

RESPONSE: For in Christ all the fulness of God was pleased to dwell.

LEADER: In Christ all things were created, in heaven and on earth, visible and invisible.

RESPONSE: For in Christ all the fulness of God was pleased to dwell.

LEADER:	Christ is the head of the body, the church; Christ is the beginning, the first-born from the dead.
RESPONSE:	For in Christ all the fulness of God was pleased to dwell.
LEADER:	Christ will reconcile all things, whether on earth or in heaven, making peace by the blood of the cross.
RESPONSE:	For in Christ all the fulness of God was pleased to dwell.

Prayer of Dedication

O Christ, in whom the fullness of the Godhead dwells, we offer ourselves to your service. Let time be blessed by your presence; let skills enrich the life of humankind. Receive what we bring as offerings to you. Make use of them and of us, for the sake of your holy gospel.

Prayer of Thanksgiving

God of the circling years, whose faithfulness spans generations, your grace and mercy continually astound us. Through Christ you have entered our world, walked where we walk, shared our infirmities, been touched by our joys and sorrows. You hear the prayers of all who bow down before you as Christ intercedes on their behalf. We can utter our halting phrases with assurance that Christ will translate the idiom, genre, and metaphors into symbols that communicate our love.

We are thankful that we need hide nothing from you. You know our longings and desires, our fears and temptations. We hear again of how Christ drew apart to spend time in prayer, his tears testifying to the frightening prospect of death. We sense the sorrow he endured, and witness his unyielding confession of trust in your will. Through him we too can endure.

We await the day when all hearts shall love you and Christ shall reign supreme. In the meantime, we shall continue to call on your guidance, for we know not what each day will bring. We shall arise with assurance that the dawn brings resurrection, and confront each moment as a time of grace. When the sun sets and our ministry is over, we pray that our efforts will be found worthy of your mercy and grace.

Index of Scripture Readings